The Unmaking of Canada

The Hidden Theme in Canadian
History since 1945

The Unmaking of Canada

The Hidden Theme in Canadian
History since 1945

Robert Chodos, Rae Murphy
and Eric Hamovitch

James Lorimer and Company, Publishers
Toronto, 1991

CANADIAN CATALOGUING IN PUBLICATION DATA

Chodos, Robert, 1947-

   Includes bibliographic references.
   ISBN 1-55028-339-1 (bound).
   ISBN 1-55028-337-5 (pbk.)

1. Canada — Economic conditions — 1945-
2. Canada — History — 1945- 3. Canada — Politics and government — 1984-* I. Murphy, Rae, 1935- II. Hamovitch, Eric.
III. Titlte   *69818*

FC630.C46 1991   971.064'7   C91-097593-0   F1034.2.C46 1991

James Lorimer & Company, Publishers
Egerton Ryerson Memorial Building
35 Britain Street
Toronto, Ont M5A 1R7

Printed and bound in Canada

Contents

Preface

In the early months of 1991, Canadians' attention was diverted from their own conflicts by the larger and deadlier one in the Persian Gulf. This is not an unusual situation. More often than not, Canadians have seen events in other countries — whether Vietnam, Iran, South Africa, Germany or the United States — as more dramatic, significant and compelling than anything going on in Canada.

In recent years, however, there have been several occasions when Canadians have run to their television sets, radios and newspapers to follow political events in Canada almost as obsessively as they followed the Gulf War. During the free trade debate in the fall of 1988, the final act of the Meech Lake controversy in June 1990, and again as the siege at Oka came to a head in September 1990, Canadians hungered for up-to-the-minute information and at the same time struggled to make sense of the information they were given. What was happening? Why was it happening? What had led up to it? What did it mean? What could be done?

In this book, we seek to deal with some of these questions. Our starting point is the perception that the periodic media events are a reflection of deeper changes taking place in this country, changes that will lead to the disappearance of Canada as we now know it and the emergence of something whose shape cannot yet be foreseen. Accordingly, this is not a book about free trade, constitutional questions, native rights, or other issues such as the deficit and the Goods and Services Tax in their own right. We are more interested in how these events relate to one another than in the events themselves. We also see the scope of the changes taking place as extending far beyond Canada, and we don't regard it as entirely accidental that Quebec's drive for sovereignty has occurred at the same time as that of most of the Soviet Union's republics or that increased economic integration in North America has paralleled the removal of barriers in the European Community.

This book is in part a sequel to *Selling Out*, published just before the 1988 election. There, we looked at the Mulroney government's record in its first term and discovered that the unifying elements in its various policies were commitment to business's immediate and narrow "bottom line" interests and disdain for any considerations that conflicted with that commitment. This orientation has been even more prevalent in the government's second term, and we see it as an immediate cause of Canada's current crisis. But we also believe that the reasons for the crisis go far beyond the actions of one government, and this is why we stress its historical and international dimensions.

After a brief survey of what happened in Canada in the pivotal year of 1990 (chapter 1), we go back to examine some of the major developments of the postwar period (chapters 2, 3 and 4). Despite momentary hesitations, the basic thrust of that entire period was towards economic integration with the United States, and it was this process that eventually made the existing political structure of Canada untenable. The process of integration and the undermining of Canada's political structure gathered force in the 1980s (chapter 5), and we look in particular at two of the more suggestive forms that these developments took: the emergence of the Mulroney government and the growth of a new business elite in Quebec. In chapter 6 we turn to the effects of the Free Trade Agreement and to two of the issues that have arisen in the wake of the agreement: possible extension of free trade to include a deal with Mexico and the internal constitutional arrangements of post-free trade Canada. Chapter 7 pinpoints the six months following the signing of the Free Trade Agreement as the period in which the rationale for the existence of Canada as we know it was fatally weakened and examines the broader international context in which this watershed was crossed. With this background, we come back to the events of 1990 and look at some of them in more detail: the gutting of Via Rail, the demise of the Meech Lake Accord, the confrontation at Oka and the Ontario election that brought the NDP to power (chapter 8). And finally, in chapter 9, we make some suggestions about the choices that now have to be made and the ways in which the issues of the 1990s will be defined.

The questions at issue here — of sovereignty, nationhood and the role of the state — are difficult and puzzling ones, and we claim no unique competence or insight in our approach to them. We hope that this book will be one effort among many to address these questions, which must be resolved if what emerges in Canada is to be something Canadians choose freely rather than something imposed on us by forces beyond our control.

We do, however, have an unusual perspective. We are all journalists, who have covered events in Canada and elsewhere for more than two decades, and yet none of us works in the daily print or electronic media. Those media have their uses, and we depend on them for information as does everyone else. But in writing a book such as this one, our position as outsiders gives us certain advantages. We are not subject to the pressure of the weekly, daily or even hourly deadline that gives priority to finding some "new fact" regardless of its significance or for that matter its accuracy. Even more important, we long ago gave up the search for the "inside story" not only because no one ever told us anything anyway but also because the price of being privy to the inside story is becoming a conduit for what insiders want the rest of the world to hear. Many Canadians saw through this equation in the final stages of Meech Lake, and many more people saw through it as it happened on a much larger scale in the Gulf. So our sources are public ones; those we have found most useful are listed in the bibliography at the back.

The journalist who penetrated most deeply into the truth about public life in the United States in the 1950s and 1960s was an outsider working from public sources, I.F. Stone. We would not like to carry the comparison between our work and that of a giant such as Stone too far, but we and other journalists working as we do are deeply in his debt.

Robert Chodos
Rae Murphy
Eric Hamovitch

1
—

The Crisis of Canada's Existence

In 1990, many of the assumptions on which the political entity called Canada have been based — about federalism, about relations between the two major language groups, about the proper place and role of native people, about responsible government and the powers of the two houses of Parliament — would be subject to, and often buckle under, severe stress. But what would prove to be one of the most eventful years in Canadian history began with the country in a flutter over a train.

The train was the Canadian, once the jewel of Canada's passenger fleet but lately little more than a down-at-the-heels reminder of its former glory. More than any train, the *Canadian* had symbolized the Canadian Pacific Railway's central position in Canada's national myth and its promise to maintain railway service "forever." Actually, when the CPR put the *Canadian* into service in 1955, rail passenger service in Canada was already in decline, but introduction of the gleaming stainless steel transcontinental train helped mask that fact for another decade or so. In the late 1960s, Canadian Pacific and Canadian National Railways began serious efforts to get out from under their obligation to provide passenger service, setting in motion a self-perpetuating cycle of service cuts, reductions in ridership and growing deficits. Assignment of passenger service in 1977 to a new government-owned corporation, Via Rail Canada Inc. (without any clear legislative framework and with hardly any rolling stock built more recently than the *Canadian*), briefly reversed the fall in passenger train use but made little long-term difference.

In 1989, with passage of the Canada-U.S. Free Trade Agreement out of the way, the government of Prime Minister Brian Mulroney decided that its chief priority was reducing the large and persistent federal deficit. Via Rail, running up hundreds of millions of dollars in losses while serving only a relatively small number of Canadians, was a natural target for the budget cutters in Michael Wilson's finance department. In October, the government announced the abandonment of roughly half of Via's remaining network, including the *Canadian*'s historic route along the shore of Lake Superior and across the southern prairies. The cuts were to take effect on January 15, 1990.

Even though relatively few Canadians actually ride passenger trains, the prospect of losing a large number of them was not, on the whole, popular. Petitions and demonstrations were organized. In early January, the *Canadian* made its final voyage along its traditional route, and the media clambered on board. Newspaper reporters covered each leg of the trip. CBC television's *The Journal* ran nightly clips of Canadian writers in each major city delivering sad comments as the *Canadian*'s whistle sounded for the last time.

Nothing lasts forever, and when one looks at some of the needs in today's society, it seems hard to justify federal subsidies for the opulent lounges and palmy dining cars and cosy sleepers still found on some long-distance trains. And it is easy to heap scorn on those millions of Canadians who romanticize trains but don't actually ride them. Nevertheless, as an exercise in public policy, the Via Rail cuts were a failure on at least two levels. First, the government did not make a convincing case that the cuts made sense even in strictly economic terms. And second, in a country whose component parts are tied together only by tenuous bonds, such apparently trivial links as passenger rail service had a symbolic importance that the government never managed to understand.

In the early days of Year Two of the Era of Free Trade, with north-south economic links (and Canadians' unease about their possible political and cultural consequences) stronger than ever, this symbolic importance had intensified — as had the government's incomprehension. As a result, the media laments and expressions of public anger had become a requiem not for the *Canadian* alone but for Canada.

The Year the Assumptions Collapsed

While the issue of the gutting of Canada's passenger train system came to a head in early 1990, the failure of public policy that led to it stretched back for decades. What would make 1990 extraordinary was that a number of such longstanding policy failures would come to a head one after the other. Taken together, these crises represented no less than a challenge to the foundations of Canada as a country.

Railways have, of course, played a disproportionate role in Canada's history and are disproportionately prominent in Canadians' consciousness. In standard versions of Canadian history, the story of building the nation and the story of building the transcontinental railway are one. From there, it is no great leap of the imagination to equate tearing down the railway with tearing down the nation, or at least an essential part of it. It is perhaps symptomatic of the weakness of the current federal government that it did not understand that equation. If it had, the $600 million annual subsidy to Via might not have loomed so large in its mind. The government might have understood that Canada, of all countries, cannot be run according to strict business logic — that to subject Canada to the logic of the bottom line is, in effect, to dismember it. It may well be that passenger trains make little economic sense outside the most densely travelled corridors. But economic sense cannot be upheld as the sole criterion in public policy formulation; if it were, the armed forces would have to be abolished, to take one example.

The political storm caused by the Via cuts was intense but brief. The abandoned trains were soon forgotten by everyone except inveterate railway riders, or former railway riders thrown onto overcrowded highways by the cuts. Perhaps the government was right. A train, in the end, is only a train.

In January 1990, perception of the seriousness of Canada's looming constitutional crisis was not widespread. A disastrous federal-provincial conference in the fall of 1989, highlighted by an acrimonious exchange between Prime Minister Mulroney and the new premier of Newfoundland, Clyde Wells, had raised in some minds the very real possibility that the Meech Lake Accord would not meet its three-year ratification deadline, which loomed in June 1990. At this point, however, only a small part of the political trauma that the country would undergo in the process and the deep division between Quebec and the rest of Canada that would be revealed were visible. Resolutions declaring Sault Sainte-Marie, Thunder Bay and dozens of other Ontario towns and cities English-only territory, the reemergence of the sovereignty option as a major political goal in Quebec, the spectacular resignation of Lucien Bouchard from the federal cabinet and the formation of the Bloc Québécois, the week-long, closed-door, "roll of the dice" first ministers' meeting that produced what at first appeared to be a solution but in the end turned out to be only an agreement to disagree, Native MLA Elijah Harper's refusal to allow the accord to proceed in the Manitoba legislature, the Bloc Québécois's landslide byelection victory in a downtown Montreal riding — all this was still to come.

Even as the crisis escalated, foreign observers would comment on how peacefully and politely Canada was unravelling. Elsewhere, they would note, grave threats to the very existence of a country were measured not in municipal resolutions, federal-provincial standoffs and parliamentary filibusters but in tanks, machine guns and armed clashes. As it turned out, they would only have to wait around a few months to see those as well.

If only a minority of Canadians sensed the extent to which Quebec-Canada relations as they had been understood in recent decades were coming apart, perception of an impending crisis in relations between Canada and its native inhabitants was virtually nonexistent, at least in white Canada. Native issues were easily pigeonholed and were not dealt with in the context of serious politics. In the 1960s, this longstanding view was expressed by the Royal Commission on Bilingualism and Biculturalism, which undertook a broad reexamination of how Canadian society is constituted. The B and B commissioners framed the problem posed by native peoples as "the integration of the native populations into Canadian society" and placed this problem outside the commission's terms of reference. More recently, a series of first ministers' meetings on native self-government had ended in failure in 1987, only weeks before the meeting at Meech Lake with its historic agreement.

In 1990, however, Elijah Harper's refusal to allow that agreement to proceed without native consent would put native issues squarely onto the public agenda, and the shoot-out between Mohawks and the Sûreté du Québec and the attendant blockade of the Mercier Bridge into Montreal would make it highly likely that they would stay there. Nor could these issues now be approached, as the 1960s B and B Commission had approached them, in terms of "integration" into Canadian society. Rather, native people understood the question as one of running their own affairs — in other words, a question of sovereignty.

This question of sovereignty represents a common element in the Quebec-English Canada standoff over Meech Lake and the native-white standoff at Oka. Not long before, Canadians had gone through another traumatic debate on a question of sovereignty, in this case the sovereignty of Canada itself. Just how much of it would Canada be giving up if it signed the Free Trade Agreement with the United States? The federal election of 1988 had resolved the debate in favour of the agreement, but many of the doubts remained. On one level, these doubts were fostered by economic developments in the early months of the agreement. Some of the fears expressed by the deal's critics materialized in the form of plant closings and takeovers. Some of the promises expressed by its supporters failed to materialize as a higher Canadian dollar wiped out many of the benefits of tariff reduction. Canadian imports still faced protectionist measures in the United States, and the thorny question of subsidies remained to be resolved. In 1990, a proposal for a free trade agreement between the United States and Mexico would introduce a new element of uncertainty into Canada's economic prospects.

On another level, Canada was living through the aftermath of the way the decision to proceed with the Free Trade Agreement had been made. During the 1988 campaign, the question of the survival of the country had been posed in stark terms, and the side whose project was said to threaten its survival had won. Some of that may have been overblown campaign rhetoric, but while the political mood in Canada through much of 1989 was eerily quiet, the question of the fragility of Canadian sovereignty had not been permanently laid to rest, and an inchoate sense that an essential part of the logic of the existence of Canada had been removed would underlie the crises that erupted in 1990.

Worse yet, opposition to the Free Trade Agreement on nationalist grounds was confined almost entirely to English Canada. What opposition there was to free trade in Quebec was argued strictly on economic grounds. While Quebecers saw nothing incompatible with their identity in closer economic and even political ties between Canada and the United States, English Canadian nationalists regarded resistance to such ties as a central part of *their* identity. The key element in the Conservatives' 1988 election victory was their sweep of Quebec, which was one of only two provinces to give the Tories a majority of seats. Virtually the whole difference between Pierre Trudeau's majority election victories in 1974 and 1980 and Brian Mulroney's victory in 1988 was that Quebec had turned from the Liberals to the Tories. To some English Canadians who had once been sympathetic to Quebec nationalism, Quebec's failure to return the favour represented betrayal.

At the same time, events in Europe — where the idea of sovereign states as we currently understand it first came from — suggested that the whole notion of sovereignty might be undergoing a redefinition. The sudden discovery in East Germany that its apparently solid state structure was built on quicksand, the war of nerves between Lithuania and Moscow and the declarations of sovereignty in other Soviet republics, the increased fragmentation of Yugoslavia, and at the same time, the growing consciousness of a single western European entity as the European Community prepared to dismantle interstate economic barriers by the end of 1992 — all this suggested a profound shift on an international scale in the relationship between the sovereign state as it has been defined and entities both smaller and larger than itself. Nor was there much reason to believe that Canada would be immune from the effects of such a shift. In fact, because Canada's relations both with its neighbour to the south and with smaller collectivities within the country have always been problematic, it is hardly surprising that Canada should be one of the countries to feel those effects most strongly.

Another shift underway in 1990 was a redefinition of the role of government and widespread uncertainty about just what that role is. This shift had begun in the 1980s with what became known as the Conservative Revolution, based in the philosophy that the best government is the least government and that private enterprise should be allowed free rein. In Canada, this revolution reached maturity only in 1989, with the passage of the Free Trade Agreement and the unveiling of an economic agenda in which deficit reduction took precedence over all other considerations. It is noteworthy that this agenda had played no part in the Tories' 1988 election campaign, which focused on the benefits of free trade and "managing change." But in the era of the Conservative Revolution, winning an election was one thing, and governing quite another. As soon as he had completed his task of keeping the Tories in power in 1988, Brian Mulroney retired to the wings and left the job of governing in the hands of others, notably Finance Minister Michael Wilson. Another common element in the crises of 1990 was the virtual absence of the prime minister. Even in the case of Meech Lake, the initiative with which he was most closely identified, Mulroney let matters drift for months without making serious efforts to build political support for the accord in English Canada and emerged only to make his last-ditch, and ultimately unsuccessful, attempt to patch together a deal with the premiers.

The Conservative Revolution appeared to reach its apogee in 1989. The collapse of Communist regimes in eastern Europe and their successors' eager embrace of the free market led American neoconservatives to declare a victory for capitalism in the Cold War. But in 1990, large cracks began to show, at least in Canada. The Tories sank to historic lows in the public opinion polls — lows that would suggest that what was at issue was not merely the performance of one specific government but the legitimacy of the federal government itself. Ontario voters got rid of David Peterson's Liberal government with an enthusiasm rooted less in anger at the Peterson government in particular than in dissatisfaction with the way all governments were governing. The victory of the Ontario New Democrats signalled the end of the Conservative Revolution in Canada, but of all the reasons advanced for the moderate left's dramatic reentry onto the political stage, endorsement of its program would be among the least plausible. Meanwhile, the centrepiece of the Tory economic agenda, the Goods and Services Tax, proved deeply unpopular, and in desperation people placed their hopes for defeating it on the normally ignored, unelected Canadian Senate, in a struggle that created some exciting moments as the implementation date of January 1, 1991, approached.

All these gathering crises contributed to the unease that Canadians felt at the beginning of 1990 and that manifested itself in the uproar over the *Canadian*. None of the assumptions about Canadian politics that had held sway since the end of the Second World War could be counted on to be true any more, but new ones had not yet emerged to take their place. With its corporate agenda, the Mulroney government had launched an assault on those assumptions, and people were angry at the Tories for that, but they sensed that the old structure was indefensible anyway and that the Liberals or New Democrats would not have much greater success in making it work. In the following pages, we will look at the assumptions that governed Canadian politics in the postwar era, how those assumptions were undermined in the 1970s and 1980s, why they collapsed in 1990, and what might emerge out of the wreckage in the future.

2

The Natural Governing Party (1945-1957)

To understand how the governing assumptions of Canadian politics unravelled in 1990, it is worthwhile to recall the development and expression of these assumptions and how the Liberal Party was more or less (usually less) able to reflect them and maintain itself in power throughout most of our modern history, thus becoming our natural governing party.

The Myth of the Welfare State

In a 1982 column, veteran journalist Bruce Hutchison identified the election of 1945 as the crucial event in determining the shape of Canada's postwar politics. Recalling the later war years, Hutchison wrote: "Then as now, a Liberal government read the public opinion polls and found that if things didn't change pretty soon, it could not be reelected. The Liberal, the Conservative, and the left-wing CCF parties were running neck and neck. So Mackenzie King decided to reverse the laissez-faire ideology of a lifetime. He promised a postwar welfare state and, reelected in 1945, established it."

It wasn't, of course, quite as simple as that. If it was merely a matter of poll watching, it would have made just as much sense to project a business approach to preempt the badly divided Conservatives. There would have been much support for that option in the King cabinet. In what has been described as the strongest cabinet in Canadian history, two of the strongest ministers, J.L. Ilsley, minister of finance, and C.D. Howe, minister of almost everything else, opposed any measures that could possibly be linked to the "welfare-state" discussions developing in Britain around the 1942 Beveridge Report.

The Beveridge Report, commissioned by the British government during the darkest days of the Second World War, had a profound effect on the strange man who was Canada's prime minister. William Lyon Mackenzie King saw the report as a vindication of his own approach to social welfare, as outlined in his 1918 book *Industry and Humanity*. He was also encouraged by a conversation with Franklin Delano Roosevelt in late 1942. He recalled the president remarking that "the thought of insurance from the cradle to the grave ... seems to be a line that will appeal .... [We] should take that up strongly." Mackenzie King did and commissioned his own version of the Beveridge Report.

The Marsh Report on Social Security for Canada was published in March 1943. The report suggested improvements in the system of old age pensions and the recently enacted unemployment insurance plan. Projecting a "charter for social security for the whole of Canada," it outlined plans for health insurance — first promised by the Liberals in 1919 — and a family allowance scheme. While the report was seen by some as a blueprint for postwar Canadian socialism, it was recognized by more sober critics as a means to prevent any such thing from happening. As the *Canadian Forum* editorialized, the Report on Social Security for Canada was "the price that Liberalism is willing to pay in order to prevent socialism."

The irony that King could praise himself in his diaries and in several public utterances for his prescience in 1918 and his bold humanitarian instincts in his leadership campaign in 1919, while forgetting about the whole area during the intervening period, most of which he spent as prime minister, was quite lost on him. Indeed, as historian J.L. Granatstein points out, King brooded through almost three years on the best time for a general election: for a tired government with an unpopular leader facing a bitterly divided country, united perhaps only by the sacrifices of the war and its recollection of the Great Depression, any election any time was to be dreaded. And as King brooded, he backtracked, contradicted himself and generally vacillated about whether and to what degree he should advance social welfare initiatives when the inevitable election was eventually called.

The mood of the country was clear. As historians J.L. Finlay and D.N. Sprague suggest, "The war bonanza seemed conclusive evidence that a modern government could orchestrate the peaks and troughs out of the business cycle.... The important point was the apparent efficiency with which government took control of collective resources and seemed to manage them competently for the shared goal of victory. Naturally, many people came to the conclusion that if a country could spend billions fighting wars and plan the economy for the good of that cause, the same bureaucracy might also control production to ensure peacetime prosperity and promote the general welfare by adding other social security programs to unemployment insurance."

During the more than thirty months that Mackenzie King ruminated on the federal election, the CCF came from nowhere to form a strong opposition in Ontario in 1943 and to gain power in Saskatchewan in 1944. But perhaps the most important signal — which reverberated not only among Mackenzie King's Liberals but even more strongly among the opposition Conservatives — was a 1942 federal byelection in the Toronto riding of York South. Considered at the time one of the safest Tory seats in Canada, York South was to be the setting for the parliamentary comeback of former Prime Minister Arthur Meighen, who was disinterred from the Senate and restored to the leadership of the Conservative Party with the idea that once in power he would prosecute the war and put Quebec in its place — that place being overseas and in uniform.

Meighen, who first made his reputation as the hard-rock cabinet minister who imposed conscription during the First World War and invoked the infamous Section 98 of the Criminal Code to smash the Winnipeg General Strike in 1919, was a direct illustration of the coming sea change in Canada. The Liberals stayed out of the byelection (in a manner of speaking), and Meighen was opposed only by an unknown CCF schoolteacher, Joe Noseworthy, who portrayed the Tory leader as wanting to fight the same war as he did the last time — and to preside over the same transition to peace. Noseworthy won the seat and Meighen was finished.

Forced into his final retirement, Meighen took the lesson from his defeat that the party should look westward for a political base. With — as he saw it — Ontario going left and Quebec staying French, a western base for the Tories, buttressed by support from the Maritimes, was the route to victory. Other Tories, however, had a different idea.

For younger Tories, the 1942 Meighen disaster meant a reassessment both of what they understood to be "socialism" and of what they envisaged as possible political survival. These Tories, prominent among whom was Frederick Gardiner, Meighen's campaign manager and later the first chair of Metropolitan Toronto, realized that the new postwar social order — if there was to be social order — required social and economic planning and an entirely different concept of government and its role in the economic and social system.

The conventional wisdom of the time envisaged a postwar Canada that would undergo a period of inflation as the world replaced and rebuilt, then a period of depression, and then somehow, if one was lucky, a return to the pre-Depression economic cycle — an idea similar, one supposes, to the more recent talk of an economic "soft landing." Such a prospect would hardly be tolerated by a generation whose hopes had been put on hold through the Depression and then the war.

The question was how to marry the impatient desires of the people with the economic realities of the system, and what was being proposed by the Democratic Party in the United States and the Liberal Party in Canada was to extend the elixir of the wartime production miracle, Keynesian economics, into postwar reconstruction.

Granatstein quotes J.M. Macdonnell, a prominent Conservative of the time who was also president of National Trust, as writing about a "New National Policy," under which the goal of social security would be reached with the state taking responsibility for providing employment at a wage that would enable all "to live in decency." In a speech to a businessmen's club, Macdonnell provided his peers with the following choice: "Would you rather adopt a policy which will retain the largest amount of free enterprise or — hand over to the CCF?"

Conservatives of the Macdonnell/Gardiner stripe organized a "thinkers' conference" in Port Hope, Ontario, in 1942.

Such initiatives are usually disastrous, but this conference inspired a subsequent leadership convention that, while it chose Meighen's desired westerner, John Bracken of Manitoba, as leader, also approved what in Meighen's mind was a dangerously opportunistic program committing the party to an election platform of full employment, collective bargaining rights, social security and medical insurance. The Tories thus envisaged an election campaign that would defeat the CCF from the left and the Liberals from the right, and to celebrate this contradiction, they changed their name to the Progressive Conservative Party.

In Ontario, provincial Conservative leader George Drew was convinced, under the framework of the Port Hope Conference and the recently adopted policy of the national party, to advance his twenty-two-point program, which became the blueprint for the Tories' remarkable four-decade rule in the province.

Federally, however, the issue was much more complex. The postwar election of 1945 can probably best be approached through the issue of family allowance. Popular opinion and pressure from some "progressive" Conservatives, notably Saskatchewan's John Diefenbaker and B.C.'s Howard Green, forced the Tory caucus to go along with the Liberals' family allowance legislation. Nevertheless, the family allowance was a subject of both an overt and a covert racist appeal by the Tories. At the height of tensions over conscription, George Drew sneered about the higher Quebec birthrate and an alleged subsidy "to one isolationist province." Charlotte Whitton, a Conservative social welfare expert, decided that the payment of a cash bonus for children would merely encourage the feeble-minded to reproduce — presumably even feeble-minded Anglophones.

Thus, the Conservatives were cast in an unbreakable image as diehard reactionaries. The patently false argument that the family allowance, and later other social legislation, amounted to a subsidy to Quebec destroyed any residual *bleu* sympathies, and Tory belief that social relationships in Quebec had not altered since the Quebec Act of 1774 rendered them impotent until Brian Mulroney was able to link Quebec nationalism with the new continentalism of the 1980s. And so Quebec was handed to the Liberals and Mackenzie King on a platter, allowing them to survive — barely — the subsequent general election.

But if the family allowance served to isolate the Tories, it did not mark the advent of the Canadian welfare state. In fact, the Marsh Report was buried: neither cradle-to-grave security as envisioned in Britain, Swedish social democracy, nor the social contract of exhausted western Europe would be part of our reality. A few bland promises in a Throne Speech, a meagre and actuarily sound unemployment insurance scheme and a family allowance payment do not a welfare state make. Nevertheless, the family allowance was important. The direct payments each family received went directly into local economies, and hardheaded Keynesian economists in Finance saw it as a means of economic stabilization after the war. It was money in the hands of those who needed it; but of equal importance, it was money in the hands of those who would spend it.

One can estimate how important a measure family allowance was and yet how far Canada remained from being a welfare state by one statistic. Before family allowance, government expenditure on health and welfare was 2.2 per cent of revenues. In 1945 it increased to 10.5 per cent. This was a dramatic increase, but hardly the millennium. Rather than establish the Canadian welfare state or move us in the direction of postwar Europe, it sealed the arrival in Canada of the American New Deal.

The potent coalition that Franklin Roosevelt created in the United States arrived in Canada on the wings of the CIO and industrial unionism. The New Deal in Canada was in many senses the social and political expression of economic continentalism. And while there are significant differences between the Canadian and American experiences, the parallels are of more importance.

During the Depression, Mackenzie King and the Liberals, both in and out of office, generally eschewed Roosevelt's economic palliatives and the "fiscally irresponsible" attempts of the New Deal to build the American infrastructure. There would be no Tennessee Valley electrification projects, no Hoover Dams. But the war, the financing of which was Keynesianism writ large, made believers out of Canadians, especially many of the brighter lights in the civil service.

In the heightened political atmosphere of the war years, the Liberals seemed increasingly torn apart or squeezed by the tensions between English and French Canada. The federal Liberal party was virtually nonexistent. Meanwhile, the CCF, which had already toned down its battle cry from the 1933 Regina Manifesto and was focusing its efforts on reforming the distribution side of the system rather than attacking its property relationships, was clearly on a roll, and the Conservatives — now Progressive Conservatives and fully committed (or almost) to a policy of full employment, collective bargaining, social security and medical insurance — were confident enough to write off Quebec and do battle with the dithering shirker Mackenzie King. As the war progressed, the prime minister made some listless attempts to revitalize the moribund Liberal Party, but without success. It was into this political vacuum that the civil service stepped, overflowing with policy ideas acquired from Keynes in Cambridge and brought to Canada by way of New Deal Washington.

The fledgling Canadian mandarinate was made up almost entirely of disciples of John Maynard Keynes. John Kenneth Galbraith, the Canadian-born economist who played an important role in the development of the Roosevelt New Deal, claims that Robert Bryce was the person who explained Keynes to the Americans. Torontonian Bryce, who studied economics with Keynes at Cambridge, worked in the American government in the early thirties, and then joined the Canadian Deparment of Finance in 1938, where he became one of the leading lights in the financial administration of Canada along with Clifford Clark, W.A. Mackintosh and Graham Towers. Together with political operators such as J.W. Pickersgill and O.D. Skelton, they formed the core of the much acclaimed Canadian civil service of the time.

Canada's New Deal

Legal scholar F.R. Scott's poem written on the occasion of Mackenzie King's death probably contains as astute an analysis of the man's politics as the many political biographies of which he has been the subject. The core of his politics was "political longevity." The aim was to get elected and then reelected and between elections not to do anything that would create an obstacle to achieving this ultimate goal.

The Keynesians in Mackenzie King's civil service provided the key to achieving his goal. And while the old man delayed and feared the postwar election, the brash mandarins preached the new economic religion to the cabinet. In *The Ottawa Men*, J.L. Granatstein describes W.A. Mackintosh bouncing ideas off C.D. Howe's head: "Some ideas bounced clear across the room." Nevertheless, the economic blueprint for postwar Canada included that basic element of the American New Deal coalition: a nascent partnership between organized labour and the government, cemented by the Order in Council that recognized the right to organize industrial unions in 1944.

With the ascendancy of the civil service mandarins, the Liberal Party went into what can be seen more than forty years later as terminal atrophy. The party didn't hold a convention between the election of Mackenzie King in 1919 and the choosing of his successor in 1948. There was a policy conference before the 1945 election at which, as Jack Pickersgill recalls, every policy resolution debated on the floor was planted by himself, another member of the civil service brains trust, or the minister of national health and welfare, Brooke Claxton. Even the 1948 leadership convention was orchestrated to the smallest detail to eliminate any policy debate. If there was no party, the civil service was more than capable of filling the policy void. In this respect, the senior civil service did not merge with the Liberal Party — it *became* the Liberal Party. The irrelevance of the political party, at least once it forms a government, can be seen as something of a Canadian acceptance of the essence of the American political model.

In many respects we were fortunate that the entry of Canada into the American orbit took place during the era of the New Deal. For the influx of these American ideas made possible the introduction of industrial unionism in the 1930s and its consolidation, at least in English Canada, in the 1940s. This movement was made more complex by the almost hysterical reaction of sections of Canadian capital — mining interests in Ontario and Quebec, for example. In this respect,

Mackenzie King's political genius of being able to walk the thin line of conflicting political interests — of his on the one hand being able to conceal, in Scott's words, what his on the other hand was doing — enabled the Liberal government to be simultaneously for and against just about everything.

To this day, we live by certain myths. We cherish the notion that somehow unemployment insurance, equalization payments and medicare keep us separate from the United States and are part of the heritage of the United Empire Loyalists. The comforting notion — to some — that Canada and the United States have developed in separate but parallel directions has recently been expressed by Seymour Martin Lipset: "The two are like trains that have moved thousands of miles along parallel tracks. They are far from where they started but they are still separated." This notion simply ignores history, economics and continental regionalism.

We bought early and enthusiastically into the American Dream and the alliance between labour and capital that was the foundation of the New Deal. But the Canadian version of the New Deal alliance did have its quirks, several of which complicated the politics of postwar Canada. In particular, American social democrats had long since given up the idea of an independent party and tossed in their lot with the Democrats, some eagerly and some reluctantly. In Canada, with some rather important exceptions (Communists, leaders of the older craft unions represented by the Trades and Labour Congress, the Catholic syndicates), most labour leaders identified themselves however reluctantly with the CCF and later, somewhat more enthusiastically, with the New Democratic Party when it was formed (initially as the "New Party") in 1959. And in contrast to the situation in the United States, Canadian left and socialist intellectuals could find no home in the Liberal Party and had to create and maintain their own structures, principally the CCF. This development continues to have ramifications today and will be examined in chapter 8.

Competing Visions of Federalism

The postwar adoption of Keynesianism by the federal government also permanently unhinged the workings of a federal system that had always been based on a set of misunderstandings.

To read an account of almost any previous period in the history of Canadian federalism is to hear an eerie echo of our present constitutional crisis: the 1860s, say, when there was widespread dissatisfaction with a constitution engineered by elites without popular consent; or the 1880s, when Premier Honoré Mercier of Quebec both comported himself as the head of a national government and acted as the ringleader of an alliance of provincial premiers; or the 1910s, when conscription revealed a deep rift between French and English Canada; or the 1960s, when the Royal Commission on Bilingualism and Biculturalism issued its famous warning that "Canada, without being fully conscious of the fact, is passing through the greatest crisis in its history." But it is to the late 1940s and 1950s that we owe the origin of our constitutional difficulties in more or less their present form.

It was believed in Ottawa that for the new conception of the state embodied in Keynesianism to work, the federal government would have to retain the new powers it had gained during the Depression and especially the war. In this schema, the primary function of provincial governments was to get out of the way. Unemployment insurance was added to federal powers by constitutional amendment in 1940, as were old age pensions in 1951. But the federal Liberals' "new national policy" was resisted, naturally enough, by some of the provincial premiers of the day, notably Maurice Duplessis of Quebec.

Of the controversies of that period, the one over federal grants to universities has lasted longest in the Canadian political memory, mostly because of the famous essay on the subject by Pierre Elliott Trudeau, in which he, well-known as an anti-Duplessis polemicist, took the premier's side in opposing the grants — an indication of the breadth of Duplessis's support on the question. It was accompanied by an equally fierce struggle over taxation, with Ottawa seeking to maintain its wartime monopoly over income taxes. Duplessis said no, and eventually went on the offensive by imposing his own provincial income tax. At the time, this was regarded as inadmissible in Ottawa because it meant that federal tax law would be applied differently in Quebec than it was in other provinces, giving Quebec a form of special status. In Quebec, the tax controversy was important not only in itself but also because it served as the occasion for a provincial royal commission, the Tremblay Commission, that produced a detailed and influential report buttressing Quebec's pro-autonomy position.

To note that the federal government that carried out most of these centralizing initiatives was headed by a French Canadian prime minister and supported by a solid phalanx of Liberal MPs from Quebec should be sufficient to avoid the temptation to see these controversies simplistically as a French-versus-English conflict. It is nonetheless true that the goals of Canadian federalism were seen very differently in Quebec City than they were in Ottawa, and the provincial government's stance had widespread support among Quebecers. Indeed, while most aspects of Duplessis's system crumbled soon after his death, the defence of Quebec's autonomy was not among them, and even Quebecers who had fiercely opposed Duplessis's authoritarianism, corruption and servility to corporate interests would grudgingly acknowledge his achievements in this area.

The competing views of the federal system were old, dating back to the Confederation period, but they acquired new significance with the expansion of government activity. And even though the specific controversies that had pitted Duplessis against Saint-Laurent were settled fairly amicably in the late 1950s, jurisdictional struggles between the two levels of government were only beginning.

Canada in the American Century

Welcoming Prime Minister Brian Mulroney's decision to join the Organization of American States as long overdue, the old Liberal warhorse and former minister of external affairs, Paul Martin, Sr., recalled urging Canada to join the OAS's predecessor organization, the Pan American Union, in his maiden speech to the House of Commons in 1935. If Martin's leader at the time, Mackenzie King, was listening, he wasn't buying the notion. King at that time was acting as his own minister of external affairs — many people believe he did so just to make certain Canada didn't have any — and was wary enough of our membership in the League of Nations.

For King, involvement in European affairs spelled only trouble and risk for our fragile unity without any compen-

satory benefit. As King grew older, his fear for Canada's safety
in foreign entanglements and his sense of powerlessness to
prevent them led to a schizophrenic policy. King reinvented
the British Commonwealth while simultaneously hastening
the time when it would be forever irrelevant to Canada. He
negotiated free trade with the U.S., finally rejected it, and all
the while encouraged the process that would make it inevitable. He was determined to take the credit for being one of
the founders of the United Nations but was fearfully reluctant
to participate in it. In his last years, the grandson of the
Yankeephile rebel of 1837, William Lyon Mackenzie, became
a monarchist who was apparently known to the royal family
as Uncle Rex.

However, the Pax Americana of the early years of the Cold
War held no fears for Louis Saint-Laurent, the rich French
Canadian corporate lawyer who was Canada's postwar external affairs minister and eventually King's ordained successor.
In External, Saint-Laurent and his deputy, Lester Pearson,
were key players in the formation of the North Atlantic Treaty
Organization. Much of their manoeuvring was done either
behind Mackenzie King's back or with his deliberate refusal to
know what was going on. In domestic affairs, postwar reconstruction and the conscious determination to develop our
economy as a resource hinterland were left completely in the
hands of C.D. Howe. Tory publisher Grattan O'Leary recalled
asking the retired C.D. Howe how he was able to get away
with his policy while Mackenzie King was still prime minister.
Howe replied that King simply "didn't understand what I was
doing."

What King knew or didn't care to know and what he understood, misunderstood or chose to ignore are perhaps mere
esoteric concerns now. What is clear and significant is that
when the sick, lonely and disillusioned old man retreated to
Kingsmere in November 1948, his successor, Saint-Laurent,
was much more sanguine about the new world order, and
along with his key cabinet members, C.D. Howe (soon to be
referred to as CEO of Corporate Canada) and Lester Pearson,
did not share King's doubts about the American Century and
Canada's role within it.

With the Truman Doctrine, which pledged U.S. military and economic power to contain communism everywhere; soon to be reinforced by Secretary of State John Foster Dulles's rollback of communism, our line of march in international affairs was clear and sure. The postwar industrial boom was extended by the Korean War, and Canadians thrived not merely as hewers of wood and drawers of water but also as bankrollers of industrial branch plants, fabricators of aircraft and ships, and automobile manufacturers to the Commonwealth and Empire. There would be a price to pay, but that would be much later. In the meantime we could use American capital, American knowhow and above all American markets to build a Canadian industrial infrastructure on the sale of our resources and energy. There were limits, however, to the terms the Canadian government, if not Canadian business, would accept — limits that would not be crossed until the late 1980s and the Free Trade Agreement.

A case in point was the construction of the natural gas pipeline in 1956. The Canadian consortium wanted to build the pipeline through the United States, with small feeder lines coming up into Canada. But C.D. Howe, generally known as the prime promoter if not the grand designer of Canadian continentalism, insisted that the pipeline be all-Canadian. He demanded that the pipeline go over the Rockies to British Columbia and that the eastern section be built in Canada. In 1953, Howe defined the policy of the government: "To refuse permits for moving natural gas by pipeline across an international boundary until such time as we are convinced that there can be no economic use, present or future, for that natural gas within Canada."

Howe was so determined that the gas remain in Canada to fuel the Canadian economy that he was even willing to consider some form of public ownership — an awesome concession from his point of view but, interestingly enough, one he was willing to make on many occasions when he thought the national interest required it. It is sometimes worth reflecting on the actions of this "continentalist" as we listen to his successors (such as Marcel Masse) deny there is anything approaching the national interest in this so-called community of communities and as we see the Free Trade Agreement make it illegal for any Canadian agency to require would-be gas exporters to show that proposed exports to the United States would never create supply problems in Canada.

As it happened, public ownership was unnecessary, as a Texas oilman friend of Howe's agreed to build the pipeline through the Canadian Shield down to southern Ontario and on to Montreal. True enough, the Canadian public had to pay for most of it, and in return the American consortium was willing to own it, but the cheap energy provided by the gas was later able to fuel the industrial boom in Ontario.

Louis Saint-Laurent, C.D. Howe and the new Republican administration that took office in Washington in 1953 were philosophically likeminded. They were defenders of private enterprise, the free market and every other shibboleth of the true believers. They were also willing to use the powers of government: every economic, fiscal and monetary lever existed to be pulled. And like all other free enterprisers before and since, they were blissfully unconcerned with any irony or contradiction.

One can scarcely conceive of a more enthusiastic cold warrior than Louis Saint-Laurent. Saint-Laurent's warm endorsement of all things American led him on occasion to reveal an otherwise carefully concealed Anglophobia. And in one uncharacteristically strident outburst during the Suez crisis, he proclaimed that the era of the European superman was finished. The government he led in the decade of Pax Americana abroad and McCarthyism at home was perfectly attuned to the times — so much so that in 1949 he achieved an unprecedented majority. While he lost some seats in his second election in 1953, it too was a triumphal procession. Now playing the role of Uncle Louis, he patted heads and clucked cheeks and carefully camouflaged the mean-spirited, right-wing government he and C.D. Howe controlled like a private business.

So perfectly attuned was he that he was unable to hear the discordant notes and unfocused disharmony in the country. Were Canadians becoming nervous over increasing Americanization? Was John Foster Dulles's "brinkmanship" in the Cold War beginning to rattle? Were we tiring of a government of budget surpluses that was unable to develop and expand a miserly pension and an inadequate unemployment insurance system that had to remain "actuarially sound"? And (we were rather sensitive about our institutions in those days) was there growing concern over the impotence of Parliament?

In any case, in 1957 it was time for an election. Uncle Louis was tired, ill, never an enthusiastic campaigner, and totally oblivious to and uncomprehending of the new gadget, television, but the party would have "run him stuffed" if necessary and he sleepwalked through the disaster. In hindsight, the cynical Pickersgill advanced several reasons for the defeat of 1957 — from the public's being bored with an obviously old and tired regime to the fact that Pickersgill himself, as minister of immigration, was no longer a member of Saint-Laurent's staff and was thus unable to tour with the old man and write his speeches. None of these reasons, incidentally, had anything to do with the challenger, John Diefenbaker. Indeed, Pickersgill and the other leading lights of the Liberal Party had such a low opinion of Diefenbaker that they thought he would cause the Conservatives (who otherwise deserved victory) to lose. But whatever reasons one chooses to mix and match, the Liberal defeat of 1957 and the subsequent Tory minority government were not simply the results of an upsurge of Canadian nationalism, as we tend to imagine in retrospect. Similarly, Diefenbaker's subsequent majority triumph resulted from a number of more complex considerations — and was largely fashioned in Quebec by Maurice Duplessis.

After Diefenbaker's 1958 landslide, the era of the Liberals as Canada's natural governing party seemed to be definitively over. And indeed, Liberal political dominance of Canada would never again be quite the same. But the Liberals would be back — partly because of the bumbling and incoherence of the Diefenbaker government, partly because of the rebuilding work done by such Liberals as Keith Davey, Tom Kent and Walter Gordon, and partly because the path on which the Liberals had set Canada in the postwar years had by no means reached its end.

3

Three Faces of Nationalism (1957-1968)

If the election of 1957 was at best peripherally a Canadian nationalist victory, the election of 1963 seemed much more clearly to be a Canadian nationalist defeat. Along with the struggles over reciprocity in 1911 and free trade in 1988, it was one of those rare elections fought on a clear Canadian-sovereignty-versus-continental-integration issue — in this case, the question of whether U.S. Bomarc missiles on Canadian soil should be armed with nuclear warheads. John Diefenbaker, who opposed the warheads, lost; Lester Pearson, who supported them, was elected. And yet it was this very election that gave a considerable measure of political power to the most noteworthy Canadian nationalist of the postwar era, Walter Gordon.

Diefenbaker, the prairie trial lawyer, and Gordon, the Toronto chartered accountant, represented very different strains of Canadian nationalism. In the early 1960s, another form of nationalism was also making its presence felt: the new Quebec nationalism embodied in the innovative government of Premier Jean Lesage in Quebec City. The question of how to reconcile this new Quebec nationalism with either strain of Canadian nationalism would constitute a difficult challenge for another product of the 1963 election, the Royal Commission on Bilingualism and Biculturalism, and would be a continuing if often submerged theme of Canadian politics into the 1990s.

John Diefenbaker: Canadian Populist

Social philosopher George Grant wrote an elegant eulogy for the Diefenbaker government, *Lament for a Nation*, in 1965. It serves as something of an antidote to the approved Liberal histories of the Diefenbaker-Pearson years. But when Grant portrays Diefenbaker as something approaching Canada's last best hope, the eulogy becomes a little tattered. John Diefenbaker had no clear national vision, or at least none that bore any resemblance to the twentieth century.

Diefenbaker and others like him saw British North America as a living, breathing thing — distinct from the United States by virtue of the British tie and distinct from Britain by virtue of being North American. Because the monarchy and other British institutions and symbols transplanted to Canada kept us separate from the United States, Diefenbaker saw these institutions as being of value not only to Canadians of British descent but also to those of all other nationalities, notably including French Canadians. The only Canadian was an "un-hyphenated Canadian," living under the protection of the Crown. However, although Diefenbaker has been identified with the British-leaning, anti-individualist conservatives we quaintly call Red Tories, his politics really had little in common with theirs. Diefenbaker was a populist in the great American tradition — more William Jennings Bryan than Benjamin Disraeli.

Diefenbaker was neither anti-American nor wholly mindless of changing power relationships between the United States and Britain, but he clearly either didn't understand these relationships or at the very least underestimated the change that had taken place. Thus he envisaged a great transatlantic English-speaking commonwealth with Canada as a bridge, a notion that would have been fascinating to contemplate had the American Revolution not occurred. The "special relationship" between Britain and the United States, which successive British prime ministers have revelled in and deluded themselves about, never did include Canada. At the historic 1943 meeting between Roosevelt and Churchill in Quebec City, Mackenzie King was invited along for several photo opportunities, but he was generally treated, as he once described it, as merely the manager of the host hotel. Canada's status in subsequent Anglo-American meetings hardly improved, as

Diefenbaker discovered when he arrived uninvited at a meeting in Nassau between Harold Macmillan and John Kennedy.

During Diefenbaker's term of office, Canada joined NORAD, made new defence production agreements with the U.S., dismantled its independent aircraft industry and accepted American missiles on its territory. But these actions were simply part of an inevitable process that could not have been reversed without a repudiation of our basic policy, which had been hurriedly enunciated by Mackenzie King in Ogdensburg, New York, in 1940 when the Permanent Joint Board on Defence was set up. At the time, the argument ran that a virtually defenceless Britain faced an imminent Nazi invasion, leaving an even more defenceless Canada with nowhere to turn except Washington. As a result, the United States became Canada's defender, and in the early 1960s this was still so; only the enemy had changed. But these arrangements had their costs — costs that John Diefenbaker, like other Canadians, sometimes forgot. In a sense, the process set in motion at Ogdensburg reached its culmination at the time of the Cuban missile crisis in 1962, when Canadian armed forces were put on alert by NORAD Command in direct contradiction of an order by Prime Minister Diefenbaker.

If Diefenbaker is considered a nationalist tendency within the Conservative Party, then in the 1960s and early 1970s the Conservative, Liberal and New Democratic parties all had nationalist wings contending within them and all three parties defeated those wings. But Diefenbaker's nationalism was apparent mostly in retrospect. At the time his victory was seen as a gain for the right, for the Republican Party North. The response of both the Liberals and the soon-to-be-christened New Democrats was to adopt the policies of the Democratic Party: the New Frontier and later the Great Society.

Walter Gordon: The Man Who Would Buy Back Canada

The victory of John Diefenbaker propelled many formerly nominal Liberals into public political life. Among them was Walter Gordon, arguably the most interesting political figure in postwar English Canada. In the words of his biographer, Denis Smith, Gordon was not easily drawn to politics and suffered its wounds as much as anyone: "Through it all he retained his dignity, his integrity, his generosity, and his wit." One might add he also retained his naïve belief that Canada's business class would or could assert a goal of an independent economic and therefore political entity. Born into the capitalist establishment, Gordon prospered in his own right and was in no sense an apostate. Yet in the sense that Franklin Roosevelt was seen by many of his peers as a traitor to his class when he was actually part of the system's salvation, Gordon experienced the lash of antipathy from those to whom he felt nearest and dearest, and unlike Roosevelt he never became a popular leader. His clipped moustache, "old school" bearing and droll, inflectionless speech set him not so much apart as aloof from those who shared his nationalism. It was his nationalism that drew him to politics.

Even before the war, as a successful young capitalist, Gordon worried about increasing American ownership of Canadian industry and resources. He attempted to raise capital to organize a holding company whose purpose would be to buy these enterprises from their American owners and presumably become an alternate source of investment capital in Canada. He looked to both Britain and continental Europe for investment funds. The outbreak of hostilities in Europe put an end to that scheme. But the notion of a buyback from either private sources or government, in many variations and combinations, remained a hallmark of his approach — a sort of national Fabianism.

The war also gave Gordon a chance to develop his ideas. He held several key economic posts in wartime Ottawa, and as he experienced the organization of the war effort he became a true believer in the magic power of Keynesian economics, then coming into its own. Gordon was one of those who believed that Keynes could be used in peacetime to create a strong, centralized, interventionist government that could guarantee both sovereignty and rising social standards. This was the impulse that drove him to government. Gordon had great ambitions, but unlike most Canadian politicians, he aspired to office as a means to an end, not as an end in itself. He was part of the new wave of postwar social and political engineers.

Walter Gordon was always a Liberal. He was a friend of civil service comers such as Robert Bryce and Louis Rasminsky as well as the rising diplomat Lester Pearson. He was an integral part of the relationship that has been encapsulated in a question: are all civil servants Liberals or are all Liberals civil servants? In Canada we believed we ended ideologies and politics long before American philosopher Daniel Bell discovered the end of ideology in the United States. Politics and government, at least on the federal level, were a question of administration; C.D. Howe once accused an opposition member of making a political speech in Parliament. In this context a lifelong Liberal such as Walter Gordon could easily move from business to the civil service to partisan politics without noticing any movement at all, just as a career diplomat such as Lester Pearson could move from the department of external affairs to Parliament and consider it simply a line promotion.

Louis Saint-Laurent approached Walter Gordon shortly after Pearson made his move. Saint-Laurent had a junior ministry in mind for Gordon, one in which he could be groomed. He would be part of the "Junior League," as Howe once put it. Unlike Pearson, who was very much the prime minister's alter ego in foreign policy matters, Gordon had his own cause and hoped to further his own economic agenda by being appointed to a senior economic portfolio. It was an agenda very different from that of the current boss. Gordon was not about to be groomed. As he described the scene in his memoirs, Gordon went to see Howe before making a final decision on whether to accept Saint-Laurent's offer.

Howe asked Gordon why he was hesitating about getting into politics. "Where else could I get as big a job?" Howe exclaimed. Gordon went on to tell Howe that he wasn't sure how he would fit into the government: "'If, for example, Mr. Howe, you were to bring a proposal to Cabinet and as a new member I questioned it, what would your reaction be?' His reply was one of astonishment: 'You'd do *what*, young man?' I had the answer I required. Mr. Howe was not going to change, and neither was the government."

Gordon did not join the government, but he did win a consolation prize of getting a commission to study Canada's economic prospects. The creation of the commission was seen by C.D. Howe, who considered Canada's economic prospect to be himself, as a personal insult. A preliminary report released in late 1956 reached conclusions concerning the growing danger to our sovereignty represented by American capital penetration and called for more direct government intervention in the Canadian economy and special development scenarios for the Maritimes. These suggestions enraged Howe. Many of them echoed ideas put forward by John Diefenbaker, all of which were described by Howe as "rot." In tabling the preliminary report, Saint-Laurent said that the cabinet had no comments to offer on it and should it at some later time address any of the points made in the report it would be sheer coincidence.

It was all soon to be moot. That summer the government was defeated. The final document was presented to a new government that was not going to read any Liberal propaganda even if it agreed with it. And Walter Gordon was just warming up to a subject that would consume him for the rest of his life.

The Keynesians and the Conservatives

The leading Conservative historian Donald Creighton described, or rather decried, the "new road" Canada took after the war, "the new world of planning and management, of economic controls and social equalization. Its basic principles had not been conceived by Canadians but laid down chiefly by two Englishmen, J.M. Keynes and W.H. Beveridge." Canada, Creighton thought, was by history, organization and background alien territory for these principles. Indeed Creighton, the Conservative nationalist, had no time whatsoever for the Liberal Keynesians, although he and Gordon shared many of the same nationalist sentiments. This division became especially striking during the collapse of the Diefenbaker government, which was orchestrated from the White House (we did not then have the word "destabilization"), and its aftermath. In the Conservative nationalist view, the Liberal Party is Washington's chosen political instrument; in 1965 George Grant would denounce the Liberals (along with most of Ontario) as traitors. At the same time that Grant was writing *Lament for a Nation*, Gordon, as chief organizer and economic spokesperson of the same Liberal Party, was trying to figure out how to turn the Canadian government into a gigantic holding company to eliminate American economic control.

To Conservatives such as Grant and Creighton, the Liberals were, are and always will be the party of continentalism. In a work written after Lester Pearson's retirement and long after Walter Gordon had left Ottawa, Creighton wrote that "the decline and fall of the British Empire-Commonwealth and the growth of a continentally organized North America were twin processes which had been going on for over four decades and which successive Liberal governments in Canada had actively encouraged and assisted."

The Empire would have fallen quite as easily if the Liberal Party had never been organized. But statements such as these indicate why Walter Gordon and those who shared his viewpoint in and around the Liberal Party could never make common cause with the Red Tories. They especially criticized the latest mutation of Red Toryism in John Diefenbaker as a mixture of stupidity, demagoguery, vanity and egotism. Gordon once confessed to Lester Pearson that he was never very partisan except when it came to Diefenbaker.

The ideological foundation of the "new road" was described by Tom Kent, policy adviser to Pearson and Walter Gordon's close collaborator in the Liberal revival in the 1960s, in his memoir *A Public Purpose*:

> Freedom is not just the absence of constraint but equally, the opportunity to act. For anyone except a hermit, the opportunities of the individual depend on the society in which he lives. In contemporary society, with all the interdependence that is inherent in advanced technology, much of what we can do, as consumers as well as producers, is not individual but collective. We have to make decisions about it as a society. That is to say, a good deal of our consumption necessarily takes place through expenditures of government. In this sense — not in the socialist sense that government should own the means of production — freedom for the individual does not lie in pushing back the increased role of government.

During the Diefenbaker interregnum, Kent and Gordon developed this outlook to create a new Liberal policy that promised a new range of social services, medicare, regional development and job creation programs.

After Diefenbaker's smashing victory in 1958, most practical people believed that the Liberal Party was finished for a very long time. It was reduced to forty-eight members in the 265-seat House. Moreover, the CCF, with a mere eight members, had decided to create a new, more broadly based party in conjunction with the trade union movement. The creation of the New Democratic Party was seen by the Liberals as a direct threat to their voter constituency in English Canada. Thus in a real sense, Gordon, Tom Kent, Keith Davey and a few others were given a party to play with that had no immediate prospects. It could thus develop any policy it wanted, subject to the constraint of seeing its main threat coming from the political left.

This problem for the Liberals of the early sixties was best illustrated by a "thinkers' conference" in Kingston in 1960, where Kent presented his social issues proposals and Walter Gordon rushed over to shake his hand. "Let me shake the hand that just strangled the New Party," he exulted. Meanwhile John Diefenbaker's universe began to unravel faster than anyone had a right to expect. In 1962 the Conservatives were reduced to a minority, and in 1963 they were defeated in the House of Commons.

In the runup to the 1963 election, fought on the issue of acceptance of American nuclear weapons, the Kennedy Administration gave all the assistance it could to the Liberal campaign, including the loan of Louis Harris, the Democratic pollster. Harris met often with Walter Gordon, who was running the campaign, and once mentioned that he would soon be speaking with the president and offered to transmit any message. Gordon said to tell Kennedy not to say anything about Canada or the election for the duration. Clearly Gordon felt open association with the Americans would ruin the Liberals' chances. Meanwhile, Diefenbaker's anti-American crusade breathed life into an otherwise moribund government and severely damaged the Liberals' strategy of winning segments of the broad reform "left" away from its flirtation with the newly formed NDP. Thus, Pearson's overture to Kennedy probably cost the Liberals a majority government in 1963.

The American issue put the Liberals on the defensive and was directly responsible for their desperate slogan of the final stage of the campaign: "Sixty Days of Decision." Gordon figured they needed something to give them momentum, but he thought One Hundred Days of Decision would give them more time, since no one had much of an idea about any decision they wanted to make. Pearson, the old history prof, recalled Napoleon's hundred days to Waterloo and would have none of it, so sixty days it would be.

When the Liberals won the election, Walter Gordon at last had his chance. He was appointed minister of finance, the position in cabinet he had long sought, with a mandate, he thought, to launch the economic counterattack against foreign encroachments. As the last of the Sixty Days of Decision slipped by, Walter Gordon's first budget was hurriedly prepared and delivered. There have been other disasters that have produced destruction in less time — the San Francisco earthquake, Mount St. Helens — but these have been mainly in the field of natural history.

Who Killed the Gordon Budget?

The achievement of improved relations with the United States was signalled by Pearson's quick visit to meet Kennedy at the president's Hyannisport retreat where, among other things, the new prime minister was quizzed on baseball trivia.

Announcing as Pearson was about to leave that "he'll do," Kennedy walked through the drizzling rain to the flagpole, hauled down the presidential flag and presented it to Pearson. Charles Ritchie, our ambassador to Washington at the time, recorded the event, remarking that the rain clouds seemed to part as Kennedy made that gesture. The Pearson government enhanced and developed our relationship with the U.S. by moving completely away from any of the lingering Diefenbaker notions of breathing economic life into the British Commonwealth. But Pearson's achievement of his goal was complicated by the early influence of Walter Gordon inside his government.

Walter Gordon's background was as an extremely clever and resourceful accountant. His politics were devoted to the preservation of the capitalist system in Canada. To accomplish this objective he strongly felt the need for the active intervention of a strong centralized government. Gordon well understood the true nature of a mixed economy (if not the impossibility of repurchasing Canada). He was, his quirky nationalism notwithstanding, a product of his times — the Depression, the war and, above all, the Roosevelt New Deal. All these aspects of his political persona gave a certain coloration to many of his ideas and proposals.

As a critic said about one of Gordon's books, "there is a lot of financial gimmickry incorporated in his ideas." And while many of Gordon's ideas litter the landscape of the Pearson years, most are remembered for the fact that whatever they were supposed to do, they didn't. To be fair, most of his projects looked nothing like what he had envisaged by the time they were enacted. Nevertheless, under his bland self-assurance was a bottomless well of simplistic, counterproductive and just wrongheaded ideas. A case in point was his budget, which marked a nadir (though far from the only one) in the regime of Lester Pearson.

Fearing rapidly growing American investment in Canada and the consequent steady alienation of our resources and industry, Gordon was able to do something to discourage it. He decided to tax it. His budget announced a 30 per cent withholding tax on foreign-financed takovers.

The first attack on this proposal came not from the Americans but from Eric Kierans, then president of the Montreal Stock Exchange. Speaking for himself and "the financial capitals of the world," Kierans saw the tax as an "axe to murder the record of trust and confidence between Canada and other countries." Kierans was soon joined by every other element of the business community. In the face of this concerted onslaught the Liberal cabinet and caucus crumpled, and the tax was withdrawn. So abrupt was the collapse that Colin Cameron, an NDP member of Parliament, had to admonish the government: "For heaven's sake, pull yourselves together! We cannot afford any more of these follies, any more of these ineptitudes, because the rest of us Canadians have to cringe along with you at the ridiculous spectacle you are presenting to the rest of the world."

In one stroke half of the underpinnings of Walter Gordon's political platform — that Canadian business would or could be saved from the blandishments of American capital — collapsed. What was going on in the fifties and sixties was neither rape nor pillage. It was clearly an arrangement between consenting adults. Canadian business was, in the words of one journalist, "whoring on the sidelines of the world's biggest dollar bonanza."

The problem is, as George Grant wrote in *Lament for a Nation*: "The power of the American government to control Canada does not lie in its ability to exert pressure; the power lies in the fact that the dominant classes in Canada see themselves at one with the continent on all essential matters. Dominant classes get the kind of government they want."

When news of Gordon's withdrawal of the withholding tax was flashed to the Montreal Stock Exchange, the gleeful denizens hoisted Eric Kierans on their shoulders and paraded him around the floor.

No, 1963 was not going to be a replay of the reciprocity election of 1911. For Canadian business, truck and trade with the Yankees was much to be desired. Meanwhile, another story was emerging that would destroy the remaining pillar of Gordon's economic theory: the idea that the American takeover is reversible.

During the days of the Gordon budget fiasco, the American government faced a growing crisis of capital outflow. Into President Kennedy's office strolled Defense Secretary Robert McNamara with the good news that he had found a way to cut $30 million from the overseas defence budget. Kennedy, however, was not impressed; instead, he waved a copy of the New York *Times* with an article describing a large Wall Street loan to Hydro-Quebec to finance the nationalization of Quebec's private electricity-producing firms.

Drastic action was required to protect the American dollar. Half the 1963 balance of payments deficit was accounted for by foreign borrowing in the New York money market, where Canadian firms, municipalities and provincial governments had, during during the year's first six months, sold $607 million worth of new stocks and bonds — 67 per cent of all new foreign securities taken up during that time.

The action Kennedy proposed was to raise interest rates on money borrowed in the U.S. to be invested abroad. In other words the American government was acting to discourage American foreign investment. Canada, now seen as a major part of the problem, was not to be exempt. One would think Gordon and the Canadian government would have been over-joyed. However, when they were given advance notice of the American move during a luncheon less than a week after the 30 per cent takeover tax was withdrawn, Gordon belted down his drink, bolted from the room, and with a couple of advisers in tow flew to Washington to beg exemption.

Here accounts diverge somewhat. Journalist Peter C. Newman (who describes the incident in vivid detail in *The Distemper of Our Times*) has Louis Rasminsky, then governor of the Bank of Canada, lecturing the Americans that Canada was a profit centre for the U.S. and that our trade deficit more than balanced the sale of Canadian securities to Americans. Any discouragement of Canadian borrowing in the U.S. might eventually require a reduction in Canadian imports from the U.S. The Americans responded to Rasminsky by saying they weren't aware of how integrated our money markets were and for a price they would make a separate deal for Canada.

Denis Smith, Gordon's biographer, has a somewhat different spin. He notes that the Americans may have been moved by Rasminsky's pleas but remained unconvinced. They were, however, influenced by the spreading panic on the Canadian stock exchanges and agreed on a partial exemption for Canada — one with many strings attached. While the agreement quieted the stock markets in Canada, the terms gave the president of the United States virtual veto power over Canadian monetary policy. Newman quotes some reaction to the agreement in Canada:

> "With one act," [Scott Gordon, head of the Carleton University economics department,] said, "we have put into the hands of the U.S. president more control over our economy than the past twenty years of growth of American investment in Canada represent."

> The strongest condemnation came from Fraser
> Robertson, financial columnist for the *Globe and Mail*,
> who wrote: "The major implication of the agreement
> is this: The Canadian government agrees that for the
> future Canada will be an economic satellite of the
> United States. Our financial stability, the level and
> direction of our trade, the capacity of our business
> to develop, the right of a private citizen even to take
> a trip to Buffalo, all are handed over to the safekeep-
> ing of Uncle Sam."

In the House, Diefenbaker thundered that the agreement
"leaves, as I see it, a veto with the president of the United
States with regard to the expansion of Canada's economy,
which is something that is not in keeping with the sovereignty
of this nation."

According to Denis Smith, "Walter Gordon did not need to
be told." But apparently he did need to be told. This story has
yet another twist. A few weeks later, Gordon again descended
on Washington. He met his old friend George Ball, then un-
dersecretary of state. Ball, according to Gordon, rather rudely
chastised the late Canadian budget: "His tone was heated, his
choice of language gaudy, and his facts inaccurate .... I decided to reply in the same vein. I made it clear that he had no
right to speak to a member of the Canadian government that
way."

The discussion continued, presumably on a friendlier level,
and Gordon has Ball finally admitting that he really didn't
understand the Canadian problem or viewpoint. So contrite
was Ball that during a formal dinner that very evening Ball
made a speech thanking Gordon. According to Gordon, "he
said he learned more from me about Canada than he had ever
known before."

At this point Denis Smith rather cattily raises a volume Ball
was shortly to publish. In The Discipline of Power, a few
condescending paragraphs are devoted to Canada's "rearguard action against the inevitable." The "inevitable" for Ball
was a free trade agreement, the result of which will "inevitably
be substantial economic integration, which will require for its

full realization a progressively expanding area of common political decision."

Gordon soldiered on after the budget debacle, temporarily maintained the virtual domestic monopoly for our chartered banks, and played a role in the development and implementation of many of the social reforms of the Pearson era, the last major social welfare legislation in Canada. But it was really all over for him in government as the class he sought both to represent and to convince to adopt a policy of national resistance would have none of it.

It is, however, a tribute to the tenacity of the man or perhaps better the tenacity of his ideas that Pearson was forced to keep Gordon around. Pearson first let Gordon down by refusing to defend his controversial budget and finally doublecrossed him in 1965 by promising him that he would remain as finance minister while at the same time promising the movers and shakers that Gordon would be replaced.

After resigning from cabinet and threatening to resign his seat, an act that some Liberal strategists felt would further weaken the already wobbling government, Gordon was brought back into the government as minister without portfolio. Gordon thought his role would be much bigger than it turned out to be. He was, however, again given a consolation prize, a commission to oversee. The commission finally produced what was to become known as the Watkins Report, which caused a great stir everywhere except in the Liberal government of Lester Pearson, by then in its terminal stages. Gordon tabled the report on February 15, 1968, with the usual disclaimer that it contained the views of the commission, not the government. These views were pretty much vintage Gordon. The Commission worried about the ownership, operation and control of American multinationals in Canada and again proposed the establishment of a Canada Development Corporation to promote Canadian ownership of these companies. The report was then buried somewhere in the archives of the House Committee on Finance, Trade and Economic Affairs.

Gordon resigned a few days later and continued to write books and give speeches, proposing ways and means by which the Canadian operations of huge international conglomerates could be purchased by Canadian capital. This idea seemed to

interest many Canadians, especially those without much capital. Mel Watkins, the main author of the commission report,
became an active member of the New Democratic Party, which
eventually reacted against his economic nationalism in an even
more hostile manner than the Liberals had rejected Gordon.

André Laurendeau's Unfinished Task

In 1950, a young civil servant working on background papers
for the constitutional conference of that year (they have been
going on for close to three generations) came to the conclusion
that it was best to leave Canada's constitution alone. The
British North America Act worked reasonably well, Pierre Elliott Trudeau believed, and trying to change it would be opening up a can of worms. The position taken by Premier Maurice
Duplessis in his struggles with Ottawa was, in a sense, not so
different. He based his pro-autonomy stance not on demands
for constitutional change but on the principle of respect for the
existing constitution — which, in his view, the federal government was violating through its intrusions into provincial jurisdiction.

The generation of Quebec nationalists that followed Duplessis combined his view of Quebec's autonomy with his
opponents' view of the role of the state. Yes, government intervention in economic and social affairs had to be vastly
broadened. But this intervention would be carried out primarily by the government of Quebec. Such thinking, which
was dominant in the government of Premier Jean Lesage, led
to the conclusion that Quebec was hampered by the division
of powers in the BNA Act and that this situation should be
rectified either by giving more powers to all the provinces or
by giving Quebec some sort of special status. Political scientist
Daniel Latouche has argued that the evolution of constitutional thinking in Quebec — under both Lesage and the new
leader of Duplessis's Union Nationale, Daniel Johnson —
owed much more to improvisation than to careful planning or
philosophical consistency. But the fact remains that jurisdictional battles became institutionalized and the Quebec
government, under whatever party and whichever premier,
consistently took a position involving a stronger Quebec.

The two ways in which this could come about — through special status for Quebec or through overall decentralization — were fundamentally different, and this distinction would one day become important, even if it was not always explicit or fully understood. For Quebec, however, both processes would lead to essentially the same result, and in a sense the question of how powers were divided between Ottawa and the other provinces was not a matter of great interest to Quebec.

The emergence of an assertive Quebec state and a Francophone collectivity that was not willing to accept a secondary position in Confederation rendered the old ways of doing things in Canada no longer viable. A stronger Quebec was one possible solution, and it was the one that gained the support of most of Quebec's politicians, editorialists and academics. A notable exception was Pierre Trudeau, who as a young civil servant had been skeptical of constitutional change of any sort, and who, as justice minister in 1967 and prime minister from 1968 on, became the federal government's leading spokesperson on constitutional matters. Viscerally antinationalist and seeing the Quebec nationalism of the Quiet Revolution as simply a continuation of the reactionary nationalism of Duplessis, Trudeau favoured a solution that would make it possible for French as well as English Canadians to feel at home all over Canada. The implementation of such a program involved certain ironies. First of all, Trudeau the antinationalist became the champion of policies that sought to strengthen the sense of Canadian nationality, both internally and in the area of Canada's relations with the United States. And second, Trudeau the anticonstitutionalist was led to undertake some constitutional manoeuvrings of his own, so that individual rights, including language rights, would be affirmed all over Canada.

Accommodating different visions of Canada has been part of the art of governance in this country since the 1860s. By the 1960s, for a variety of reasons — the expanded role of the state, the new assertiveness of Quebec, increased exposure (but not increased understanding) in each of the two solitudes to the views and concerns of the other — such accommodation had become extremely difficult. The competing visions were defined in diverse ways: centralization vs. decentralization, federalism vs. separatism, special status vs. ten equal provinces, biculturalism vs. multiculturalism, individual vs. collective rights, one vs. two vs. ten Canadas. These dichotomies overlapped without always coinciding, and they were more often implicit than explicit. But the controversies of the 1960s, 1970s and 1980s — whether they concerned amending formulas, Senate reform, language rights or jurisdiction over natural resources — generally made sense, if at all, only in relation to these different visions.

Once again, to see these competing visions as a question of French against English is an oversimplification. The most intense struggle of the seventies and eighties pitted a Francophone Quebecer in Ottawa, Pierre Trudeau, against another in Quebec City, René Lévesque. The same voters who elected Lévesque's Parti Québécois in provincial elections gave heavy majorities to Trudeau's Liberals in federal ones. And major contradictions and differences of vision developed within English Canada as well. Nevertheless, the idea that Quebec constituted a nation was widespread among Quebecers, both federalist and pro-independence (again, this was not new, although some of its consequences were). The corollary of this view was that English Canada was also a nation and that any arrangement to share responsibilities for the northern half of North America — whether in the form of Confederation or sovereignty-association — was, in effect, a pact between the two nations. In the dominant English Canadian view, neither Quebec nor English Canada was, in itself, a nation; the nation was Canada as a whole.

Perhaps the most ambitious attempt to deal with these underlying questions in a constructive way was the Royal Commission on Bilingualism and Biculturalism, appointed by Prime Minister Pearson in 1963. At the centre of this attempt was the commission's guiding spirit and cochair, André Laurendeau. Like Pierre Trudeau, Laurendeau was born in privileged circumstances in Montreal; like Trudeau, he was influenced by progressive Catholic thinkers such as Emmanuel Mounier and Jacques Maritain; like Trudeau, he was one of the leading voices calling for reform during the Duplessis era in Quebec. Unlike Trudeau, however, Laurendeau was a Quebec nationalist, and he remained one until the end of his life.

Not all of his colleagues on the B and B Commission shared his views, and there were tensions and differences of vision within the commission that were never fully resolved. Laurendeau believed that the commission could not carry out its mandate without engaging constitutional questions: "Special status for Quebec is a fundamental necessity: how can we manage to integrate the new Quebec that has come to the fore since 1959 without stifling it?" In this view, bilingualism in Canada made sense only because there were two vigorous unilingual societies, one of them embodied in the French-speaking majority in Quebec. While the problems of language minorities were important, primary attention had to be paid to the language majorities. This meant that the question of greater constitutional powers that would allow Quebec to protect and promote its distinct society (the B and B Commission even used the term) was at the heart of any discussion of bilingualism and biculturalism.

Other commissioners, such as Frank Scott, had a much narrower view of the commission's mandate, believing that it should address strictly linguistic and cultural questions and not political or constitutional ones. After the commission issued a strongly worded preliminary report in 1965, these divergent views underlay a continuing discussion of the form its final report should take. Should the first volume be a wide-ranging overview, carrying forward the findings and interpretations of the preliminary report, or should it be more narrowly focused and technical? The end result was a compromise: the bulk of the first volume, which was released in December 1967, was devoted to the question of official languages, but the volume also contained the "blue pages" that constituted the report's general introduction and clearly bore Laurendeau's stamp.

A few days later, Pearson announced his retirement, setting in motion the Liberal leadership campaign that brought Pierre Trudeau to power. In his private journal, whose publication in the spring of 1990 cast new light on the politics of the commission, Laurendeau reported conversations with Pearson where the prime minister expressed his willingness to consider special status for Quebec: "In a sense, he was ahead of most of us; but he sees himself as powerless to take the steps that would be necessary. He believes in a Canada based on the idea of the specific nature of Quebec, with no attempt by the other provinces to imitate its special initiatives; how to get there?" There would be no such openness with Trudeau.

In the midst of the election campaign that gave Trudeau his first majority, Laurendeau suffered a heart attack and died; the new cochair of the commission was his fellow Quebec journalist Jean-Louis Gagnon, a Trudeau ally. While the commission published many useful reports and studies (providing valuable data, for example, on the unequal distribution of income among ethnic groups, with French Canadians near the bottom both in Quebec and in other provinces), it never really pursued the task of rethinking Canada begun in the preliminary report and the blue pages. The Trudeau government implemented the commission's recommendation that Canada adopt an official languages act, but it rejected the idea of a bicultural country. The policy of multiculturalism it embraced instead, while giving Canada's "other" cultures much-needed recognition (Laurendeau too became more sensitive to this need as a result of his travels across Canada), undercut the specificity of Francophone Quebec. Resting on a much narrower definition of culture than the one favoured by Laurendeau, multiculturalism was seen by many French Quebecers as an attempt to marginalize them.

Also not pursued was Laurendeau's developing perception that the continental and constitutional dimensions of Canada's situation were inextricably linked. While the dominant thrust of Quebec nationalism has always been pro-American, Laurendeau expressed sympathetic interest in George Grant's *Lament for a Nation* and was favourable to Finance Minister Walter Gordon's attempts to reduce foreign control of the Canadian economy. "This is where our preliminary report is weak, it seems to me," he wrote in his journal after the report's appearance. "The problem of Canadian-American relations, which is vital, is barely touched." The journal, too, touches on it only lightly. But for Laurendeau even to have perceived its bearing on Canada's cultural and constitutional problems tempts one to believe that he would have pursued this crucial question had he lived.

Although he grew steadily more appreciative of the regional and ethnic diversity of English Canada, Laurendeau continued to believe that there was enough coherence to English Canada to make a binational solution (a distinct Quebec in association with the rest of Canada) possible. He also remained, somewhat self-consciously, a federalist. "It is striking to see three important events crowded into ten days," he wrote in his journal in late 1967. "The Estates General (November 22-26), the interprovincial conference in Toronto (27-30), and our report (?). In our case, I know it's a matter of chance, and I believe it is for the other two as well. It begins with traditional nationalism, broadened and spiced up to suit the times, and it ends with federalism. Should I be surprised to find myself in the latter camp? Like Pierre Trudeau, but with a very different emphasis, I defended 'federalism' against the postwar centralizers; there's nothing illogical in defending it now against separatism."

The work undertaken by Laurendeau and never completed represents one of the great lost opportunities of recent Canadian history. We could have used a better identification of how the Quebec/Canada and Canada/U.S. dimensions of our situation intersect, as noted above. We have been hampered by a lack of understanding of the perceptual chasm that separates Quebec and the rest of Canada. We needed to know not so much whether it was possible to create a unified vision of Canada (as Trudeau endeavoured to do) as whether Canada could exist as a country while encompassing more than one vision — and especially, whether it could exist on those terms in the long shadow of the United States. If Canada's continued existence is uncertain in 1991, it is at least partly because our understanding of these questions has not progressed nearly enough since Laurendeau raised them in the 1960s.

But by late 1968, the opportunity to pursue these questions in relative calm had passed. Laurendeau's death and Trudeau's ascendancy, along with the founding of the Parti Québécois and Charles de Gaulle's endorsement of a free Quebec from the balcony of Montreal City Hall, ushered in a period of polarization. The idea of a Canada that contained a strong and distinct Quebec but was nevertheless more than just a clearinghouse for competing regional interests, which Laurendeau had favoured and on which Lester Pearson had cast a benevolent eye, was being squeezed out. The journey that would end with Elijah Harper's quiet but firm "No" in June 1990 had begun.

4

Pierre Trudeau's Three-Quarter Turn (1968-1984)

*Worse still, the commendable goal of promoting freer
trade has led to a monstrous swindle, under which the
Canadian government has ceded to the United States
a large slice of the country's sovereignty over its natural resources in exchange for advantages we already
had, or were going to obtain in a few years anyway
through the normal operation of the GATT.*

Thus former Prime Minister Pierre Trudeau concluded his
essay on the destruction of Canada by his Tory successor,
Brian Mulroney, whom he dubs "the Great Helmsman." Ap-
pearing in early 1990, it was Trudeau's first substantial comment on the Free Trade Agreement, and even then it came as
an afterthought in an essay almost entirely devoted to an attack on the Meech Lake Accord and a defence of his own
constitutional position. Yet for all that, this sparse comment
accurately and adequately summarizes, even contextualizes,
the policy that Trudeau followed for a decade and a half as
prime minister and that continues to cast its shadow on
Canadian politics even now. At the core of this policy was
Trudeau's mistrust of any manifestation of nationalism,
economic or otherwise.

Calling the deal in question a "monstrous swindle" in no
way suggests that another deal would not be worth ceding
"a large slice of the country's sovereignty" to achieve "the
commendable goal of promoting freer trade." Moreover, the

placement of this comment at the tail end of an essay condemning the Mulroney government for agreeing to the devolution of federal authority across the board points to some of the key characteristics of Canadian sovereignty: its historic vulnerability in our relationship with the United States and the context in which it resides in the bosom of a central government. The fundamental rationale of an independent country north of 49 can be challenged either by a move towards greater integration with the United States or by a redistribution of political power within Canada that weakens the centre.

In Canada we do not sing of being *über alles*. We merely stand on guard over a very fragile notion that a common market between what used to be Upper and Lower Canada can create the conditions both for nationhood and for earning a living. In Trudeau's thinking, Meech Lake posed a mortal threat to this idea, and the FTA is of the same genre in that it destroys the federal economic authority. Conversely, central assertions of economic authority, such as the Trudeau government's National Energy Program, strengthen the country in relation to the U.S. while at the same time acting as a brake against internal centrifugal forces.

The idea that slices of sovereignty could be dealt away for economic advantages is of course part of any enhancement of international trade through international agreements such as GATT, but in such cases the lessening of sovereignty is mutual among all contracting states. The FTA offers no such mutuality. While Canada has lessened its capacity to protect its economy, all the significant instruments for protecting the American economy and market remain in place. In the United States, Congress is still sovereign, free trade or no free trade. Thus, while the FTA removes restrictions on the ownership and operation of banks and other financial institutions in Canada by U.S. nationals, Canadian banks enjoy no such rights in the United States because of the operation of the Glass-Steagall Act governing the relationship between banks and the securities industry. As with any other piece of American legislation, any decision to repeal that law to establish the fabled level playing field will be made by Congress and Congress alone.

Being given preference in the American market is meaningless if everyone else is given the same preference, which is exactly what the U.S. is negotiating now with Mexico and intends to arrange subsequently with the rest of the hemisphere. Moreover, the FTA assumes greater trade between Canada and the U.S. and thus less trade between Canada and the rest of the world. The sovereignty we have sliced is in fact given to the U.S. Adam Zimmerman, chairman of Noranda Forest Inc., is quoted in Randall White's *Fur Trade to Free Trade* as saying, "I did have a strong sense from the Americans we saw that their view of us in the free trade agreement [was] that we should become an appendage of the American economy and the American economic system." Just as tails do not usually wag dogs, appendages do not become full partners with the body. The implications for the Canadian federal state are clear. A future federalist, if any can exist, will no longer be able to argue that giving up the federal connection means sacrificing cheap gas. On the other hand, a future separatist, sovereignist or autonomist will be able to argue even more strongly about the redundancy of Ottawa's handling the economic interests of Quebec, Alberta, British Columbia or — especially — Ontario. That's generally the way it is with appendages.

In engaging in textual criticism of a paragraph in Trudeau's essay, we are seeking to describe the delicate economic balance Trudeau attempted to maintain during his various administrations, especially in the explosive area of government intervention in the economy. There is also a link between economic concerns and the preoccupation with Quebec-federal relations that developed in the course of his prime ministership, especially between 1980 and 1984. This link is specifically manifest in the two most controversial elements of that final term, the National Energy Program and the 1982 constitution, and in the immediate repudiation of both by Brian Mulroney, leading to the FTA and Meech Lake.

Trudeau and the Great Canadian Misunderstanding

In a curious Americanism Brian Mulroney once observed that there was a pool of anti-Americanism in Canada, but this pool wasn't deep enough to elect a dogcatcher. Although we don't elect dogcatchers, his remark reflects a certain truth. Just because most of us don't want to become American, that doesn't mean we are anti-American. And just because some of us are somewhat anti-American, that doesn't mean we want to provoke the Americans or even have testy relations with them. Mulroney wasn't our first prime minister to make improved — even repaired — relations with the U.S. part of his election platform.

Pierre Trudeau's predecessor, Lester Pearson, made repairing relations with the U.S. a goal of his first government. This goal was achieved, for the moment, by accepting nuclear weapons. When Pearson unilaterally reversed the position of the Liberal Party on this question before the 1963 election, he seemed to be in concert with majority opinion in Canada. Yet in the context of the swirling charges and countercharges between John Diefenbaker and the State Department (and a coterie of Canadian journalists who appeared to be working out of the basement of the American Embassy), the Liberals were also seen as stooges of Washington. Among the Canadians who saw them that way was the leading light of the editorial board of the Montreal magazine *Cité Libre*, Pierre Elliott Trudeau.

At the time, Pearson was trying to revitalize the Liberals' Quebec caucus, which was rotten almost to its core. Trudeau, Jean Marchand and Gérard Pelletier were slated to be the public manifestation of the "new" federal Liberal Quebec caucus. Trudeau had been flirting with the federal Liberals for a few years, mainly because they appeared to be the only vehicle through which he could fight the fledgling independence and newly revitalized nationalist movements in Quebec. The provincial Liberals were, in his mind, becoming dangerously nationalistic, and the NDP not only was an electoral-wide disappointment — it received even less support than the old CCF — but was also now flirting with "special status."

However, Marchand, Pelletier and Trudeau backed off when the nuclear position was changed. Trudeau went on to attack the Liberal caucus in general, and Pearson in particular as "the defrocked priest of peace." He wrote that he had never seen a "more degrading spectacle than all those Liberals who changed colour with their leader ... men of my generation who tremble with anticipation because they have seen the rouged face of Power." Despite his reservations about the NDP, Trudeau supported his friend Charles Taylor, campaigning as a New Democrat in Montreal's Mount Royal riding.

Two years later, the wounds opened up by the nuclear issue had healed, and Trudeau ran against Taylor in Mount Royal; this time he would be at last a Liberal. Trudeau's conversion to Liberalism has been variously described as a betrayal of his principles, as some type of Faustian exchange for political power, and simply — and most plausibly — as an acceptance of the only game in town. Trudeau's anti-Americanism as expressed in 1963 arose from, and was circumscribed by, his adherence to the peace movement and its implicit and explicit criticism of the superpowers. In other words, it was not a product of any sense of grievance that Canada's national identity was being thwarted or undermined by Yankee "manifest destiny."

Ramsay Cook described this element of the politics of Pierre Trudeau in 1968 as he entered the race to succeed Pearson: "He rejects the rhetoric of nationalism in all its forms, whether it implies a special status for Quebec or policies of economic nationalism for Canada. He instinctively asks: Will it work? He thus irritates the nationalists in all parts of Canada."

The U.S., the Cold War and nuclear warheads were of secondary importance to the internal threat posed by Quebec nationalism. So much so that Trudeau, once considered a security threat by the American government and banned from entering the United States, would one day himself be described in the Toronto *Star* as the most pro-American prime minister in Canada's history. To be fair, he was never viewed in those terms by the Americans themselves. In *The Price of Power*, Seymour Hersh describes an incident in the Nixon White House early in Trudeau's prime ministership. Someone proposes the broadening of an American policy to include the whole hemisphere: "There was an embarrassed silence throughout the room ... broken only when Nixon remarked, 'Oh ya, then we could let that fucking Trudeau grow a beard and go play with Castro.'" In any case, after a decade and a half Trudeau would be replaced, like most prime ministers before him, by a new government dedicated to repairing and improving our relations with the United States.

Trudeau's dedicated, longstanding, even obsessive opposition to Quebec nationalism was only in part a reflection of his active opposition to the Duplessis regime. Other no less active opponents of the regime became part of the nationalist and independence movements. Indeed, it was the fusion of the social democratic left with the independence movement that provided the base and breadth of the Parti Québécois. When the PQ turned against its social democratic base it was defeated, a point apparently not lost on Lucien Bouchard as he chose a trade union organizer to contest the Bloc Québécois's first byelection in the summer of 1990.

Trudeau's antinationalism thus isolated him from the left in Quebec while also reaffirming his alienation from right-wing nationalists such as Daniel Johnson. But as he drove to succeed Pearson, it also allowed him to build a strange coalition outside Quebec. In a very real sense, counterparts of his opponents in Quebec became his base of support in English Canada, where Trudeau appealed to the people who in the eighties would become known as yuppies. This urban "with it" crowd was quite frankly bored with the NDP and desperately seeking an alternative. It would be neither the first nor the last time that the left in English Canada and the left in Quebec took opposite messages from the same experience.

There is a political theory of Canada that suggests that the rock on which the country is founded is a misunderstanding and that it has stayed together as long as it has primarily because nobody has been either willing or able to clarify this misunderstanding. From the 1860s onward, English and French Canada have held different and indeed incompatible views of how the country is constituted; Canada has held together only because each side has never explained its position to the other. This basis for national existence held until the free trade debate and the subsequent Meech Lake fiasco forced a clarification and led to the great unravelling. The Trudeau experience as he achieved, held (sometimes precariously), lost and finally regained power lends credence to this theory.

Trudeau's own part in bringing this clarification and consequent unravelling about was complex. With his direct, confrontational style, he was not one to fudge his message or say one thing in French and another thing in English (as the Tories tried to do with their unfortunate embrace of "deux nations — two founding peoples" in 1967-68). In this sense, he represented a radical departure from the Mackenzie King tradition; his on the one hand knew exactly what his on the other hand was doing. They were of a piece: on the one hand, Quebec was a province like the others, which meant no tolerance for any manifestation of Quebec nationalism, and on the other hand, Canada was to be a home for all Canadians, which meant French Canadians in powerful positions in Ottawa, a bilingual civil service, and French on corn flakes boxes.

Understandably, however, not everyone was equally attentive to all parts of Trudeau's message. In English Canada, the Trudeau of 1968 became the darling of the Francophobic element in the Liberal Party and the country, which heard only that Trudeau would stand up for one Canada, like Diefenbaker before him, and put the Quebec separatists in their place. As his first Conservative victim, Robert Stanfield, ruefully put it, "He even took our traditional bigot vote from us." But when it turned out that Trudeau's single Canada included the country's first serious effort at institutional bilingualism, this element abandoned him, to the extent that nearly half the seats the Liberals won outside Quebec in 1968 were lost in 1972.

In Quebec, Liberal strength was maintained, and even augmented, right up to Trudeau's departure from politics in 1984. There were a number of reasons for this, notably including the hopelessly alien face presented by both the Conservatives and New Democrats, but the "French Power" aspect of the Liberals' strategy was undoubtedly a significant factor (even if the translation of "French Power" into French as *"le French Power"* betrayed a certain skepticism on Quebecers' part). Liberal dominance of federal politics in Quebec even survived the election of a militantly nationalist Parti Québécois government in Quebec City in 1976. Many Quebecers blithely voted for René Lévesque in Quebec elections and Trudeau in federal ones, showing not so much inconsistency as a consistency that transcended conventional political categories. While a variety of explanations were advanced for the apparent contradiction, the most plausible was that voters were simply voting for the party that best represented their interests at each level — and enjoying the spectacle as the two governments conducted a bidding war for their loyalty. Quebec's consistent support for the Liberals could thus in no way be interpreted as a rejection of nationalism; indeed, the Liberals' intolerance of Quebec nationalism would rebound to their disadvantage once Trudeau was no longer there.

Thus, the great Canadian misunderstanding was not resolved in the Trudeau era, but its terms changed. In English Canada, saving the country was reduced to signing one's son or daughter up for French immersion. Trudeau's continued unassailable majorities in Quebec were interpreted as an endorsement for the Trudeau vision of Canada, especially after Trudeau won a direct confrontation with Quebec nationalism in the 1980 sovereignty-association referendum. And the relationship between Canadian nationalism, coterminous with anti-Americanism, and support for or opposition to Quebec nationalism remained murky. Liberal nationalists saw the question as one of standing up for the Canadian state against both external and internal threats. For a smaller number of nationalists on the left, Canada's and Quebec's national affirmation were both manifestations of anti-imperialism and therefore both to be supported.

In Quebec, many people continued to view English-speaking Canada as Westmount writ large, and English Canadian nationalism as reactionary if not directly menacing when expressed as Anglophile nostalgia and irrelevant when expressed as anti-Americanism. This view was applied especially to Ontario-centred economic nationalism, Quebec's complaint about investment — foreign or otherwise — being quite simply that it did not get its fair share. In Quebec, anti-Americanism can easily be translated into a defence of English Canadian economic and commercial domination. In its most extreme form, this view led to proposals in the early seventies for a common market between an independent Quebec and the United States, put forward by economist Rodrigue Tremblay (later a Parti Québécois cabinet minister) and former Union Nationale finance minister Mario Beaulieu (later a Conservative senator).

The End of the Old Order

The years of Trudeau's first term, 1968 to 1972, were probably the last easy economic years for Canada. The economy was growing full bore on the strength of the war in Vietnam, while our social conscience was eased by our public dislike of the napalm and B-52s. But it did have a cost.

During those years, American penetration of the Canadian economy grew enormously; 1972 was the peak year for foreign ownership in Canada. Almost every sector of the economy was foreign-controlled, with the proportion of foreign ownership reaching 99 per cent of the petroleum industry and 72 per cent of the manufacturing sector. Almost 65 per cent of trade unionists belonged to "internationals" with American head offices and more than 40 per cent of our university teachers were non-Canadian. Even the National Hockey League consisted of twelve American-owned and only two Canadian-owned teams. More alarming yet, the vast majority of American investment growth in Canada — three quarters of it — did not come from outside the country but was generated from within.

The reinvestment in Canada of profits generated by the Canadian operations of the American multinationals had the effect of making our own economic activity finance the takeover of our economy. It was also an aspect of a world phenomenon, which illustrated both the power of the American economy and its vulnerability.

As John Kennedy and more particularly Lyndon Johnson widened the war in Vietnam and proclaimed the ability of the American economy to supply both "guns and butter," other countries stepped in to provide both — for a price. Just as the earlier war in Korea provided the impulse for the Japanese economic miracle (Toyota, for example, was about to declare bankruptcy and dissolve when it received its life-saving order for trucks and jeeps from the American military for delivery to Korea), so also were Japan and western Europe prepared and positioned to make money on America's latest Asian war. Canada benefited too, as Canadian sales to the U.S. of arms and other goods the Americans needed increased dramatically with the escalation of the Vietnam War. Paul Kennedy describes this complex economic process in *The Rise and Fall of the Great Powers*:

> Both Kennedy and (even more) Johnson were
> willing to increase American military expenditures
> overseas, and not just in Vietnam, although that con-
> flict turned the flow of dollars exported into a
> flood.... The result was year after year of federal
> government deficits, soaring price rises, and increas-
> ing American industrial uncompetitiveness .... In
> the same period the U.S. share of the world (non-
> Comecon) gold reserves shrank remorselessly, from
> 68 per cent (1950) to a mere 27 per cent (1973).

The American economic crisis, which gave the lie to the
appearance of omnipotence, had been apparent even before
the carefully constructed postwar financial order, the Bretton
Woods Agreement (which provided for stable exchange rates
and established the International Monetary Fund and the
World Bank), finally collapsed in the 1970s. As we have seen,
Kennedy tried to stanch the outflow of American capital in
1963, and doing so would be even more of a concern for Johnson. However, for Canada, none of these measures were as
draconian as what was coming under Richard Nixon, and, of
more importance, we were always made exempt from their
real bite. With the Nixon shock all this would change. Canada
was thus to become one of the few economic satellites ever
given its marching papers by the boss. We often used to com-
plain about being the only country with its constitution en-
shrined in another country's Parliament. We now were in the
unique position of having our declaration of independence
read to us by another country's president.

"Nixonomics" was announced to the world in August 1971.
It included a 10 per cent import surcharge to discourage exports to the U.S. and a new tax scheme called the Domestic
International Sales Corporation (DISC), which provided incentives for American multinationals to export from American
facilities rather than import from their branch plants. Nixon
also proposed that Canada raise its dollar above par. He had
planned to cancel the Auto Pact as well but was talked out of
it a few hours before making his announcement. But there was
no talking him out of the key feature of Nixonomics, at least
as far as Canada was concerned: we were on our own. We

were now, in the eyes of Washington, a foreign country *comme les autres*. And contrary to all folklore and fable, we did not like it at all.

The Nixon shock did spark some activity in Canadian circles. We tried to define a "third option" — some sort of associate membership in the European Community. But most of all we tried to stare down the Americans: they weren't going to declare Canadian independence without a fight. Fortunately for us, other matters intervened. Treasury Secretary John Connally, no friend of Canada, resigned, and Nixon was soon to become enmeshed in Watergate and had no time for either economics or Canada.

Yet for all that, the real message of the seventies was lost on neither the American nor the Canadian government. The old economic order had broken, and something new was being erected in its place. Japan and Europe were becoming powerful centres; the United States, still the world's economic powerhouse, had priorities to shift and more than its damaged psyche to repair in the post-Vietnam era.

The period between the fall of Saigon and the rise of Ronald Reagan was a time when American power appeared to be at a low ebb. There was the Arab oil boycott, followed by the Arab buyout. There were the ubiquitous Japanese cars, cameras and VCRs. Even Canada seemed to be thumbing its nose not only at the United States but at the whole free world. Thus Prime Minister Trudeau's year-end statement in 1975 that "the free market system" didn't always seem to work. This observation of the obvious brought forth a new wave of charges that the prime minister was now emerging from the political closet as a full-blown communist ideologue. Columnist Anthony Westell finally had to put some perspective to Trudeau's remarks and in so doing summed up the total range of the prime minister's economics:

> The alarming thing about Prime Minister Pierre Trudeau's talk of new values and a new society is not that he has some secret plan to create a Socialist or corporate state but that he has no idea where he is going....

> Prime ministers are supposed to have a master
> plan, or at least a program for the next few years.
> They are supposed to have a political philosophy....
> But Trudeau has been forced to throw his pro-
> grams into reverse, and it's hard to detect any
> philosophy, whether to the left or right, beyond the
> vague commitment to brotherly love and the free-
> dom of the individual.

And so the Trudeau government drifted towards defeat in
1979. Trudeau biographers Stephen Clarkson and Christina
McCall regard the brief nine months in opposition as a period
of catharsis for Trudeau, and they see the politician who re-
emerged as prime minister in 1980 as being very different from
the Trudeau of the seventies. This may well be so; it is undoubtedly also true that he faced very different circumstances.

Listless economic negotiations between Canada and the
U.S. had begun after the inauguration of Nixonomics in 1971,
and one can draw a continuous line from these early talks to
the conclusion of the Free Trade Agreement in 1988. But it was
only after the militant nationalist administration fronted by
Ronald Reagan took office in 1981 that the negotiations became
direct and biting as American needs and demands became
explicit. Issues of the nation and economic issues merged in
the United States. In Canada, where much of the 1970s was
spent worrying over internal power relationships as expressed
in constitutional matters, a merger of economic and national
issues also developed, all of which had to do with the changing
fortunes of oil in Alberta, René Lévesque in Quebec, and Pierre
Trudeau in Ottawa.

Canada's One and a Half Nations

With the election of Lévesque's Parti Québécois government
in November 1976, the question of constitutional change acquired a new urgency, expressed in a seemingly endless series
of constitutional conferences, commissions, white papers and
resolutions. In proposing sovereignty-association, the PQ was
implicitly assuming that the rest of Canada constituted
another entity that Quebec could associate with. In this sense,
sovereignty-association was only a variant of the old two-

nation view of Canada. But while the existence of a Franco-phone nation in Quebec was no longer open to much doubt by 1976, the rest of Canada was riven by cleavages that were deep enough to make bringing all its diverse elements under the umbrella of a single Anglophone nation a very difficult enterprise.

To start with, there were the First Nations, who were beginning to force white Canadians to take them more seriously than they had in the past. As recently as 1967, the B and B Commission had dismissed native issues as of no account in its broad reexamination of Canadian society:

> We should point out here that the Commission will not examine the question of the Indians and the Eskimos. Our terms of reference contain no allusion to Canada's native populations.... The integration of the native populations into Canadian society raises very complex problems. The process of integration calls into question the very nature of the traditions and customs of native society. The Commission realizes that it was not the Government's intention ... to have the Commission undertake long studies on the rightful status of the Indians and the Eskimos within the Canadian Confederation; other bodies, whether official or private in nature ... have been entrusted with the research required for the making of government policy.

Similarly, in André Laurendeau's private journal native peoples rated only a brief and somewhat patronizing mention. But for a number of reasons — the vigorous and negative native reaction to the integrationist federal white paper of 1969, the slow progress on land claims, the encroachment of large development projects on native lands in the north, the rise of a new native leadership — as the 1970s progressed they could no longer be dismissed in the same fashion, and their political strength grew to the point where they were able to gain recognition of aboriginal rights in the constitution of 1982.

There were also the millions of Canadians whose families had come to Canada from countries other than Britain or

France. Many of them sought to retain at least some elements
of the cultures that they brought from those countries, and the
validity of these efforts was increasingly recognized at the
official level. A combination of these groups' assertiveness at
the time of the B and B inquiry, the Trudeau government's
desire to blunt the distinctiveness of Francophone Quebec, and
crass electoral calculation led Ottawa to abandon the bicultural
model made explicit in the B and B Commission's mandate
and embrace multiculturalism instead, complete with a minister of state for multiculturalism starting in 1972. Canada was
also becoming even more ethnically diverse than before, as
changes in immigration policy in the late 1960s led to increasing numbers of immigrants coming not from Europe but from
south Asia, the West Indies and other parts of the world to
whose populations Canada had traditionally been closed.

But the most serious cleavage in non-Francophone Canada
was regional. Both western and Atlantic Canadians harboured
longstanding regional grievances, and "western alienation"
became almost as ubiquitous a catchphrase as "What does
Quebec want?" Politically, western sentiments were expressed
in almost total rejection of the Liberal Party in every federal
election from 1972 on. When the economics and politics of
energy became one of the major global issues of the 1970s, the
regional dimension of the issue assumed extraordinary prom-
inence in Canada, and Alberta's Peter Lougheed became the
prototype of the regionalist provincial premier. While Americans cursed the Arabs of Abu Dhabi and Dubai, Ontarians
cursed the "blue-eyed Arabs" of Edmonton; Albertans, for
their part, were just as happy to "let the eastern bastards freeze
in the dark."

The impact of these cleavages on Quebec was felt in contradictory ways. On the one hand, they undermined the essentially dualist model of Canada to which all Quebec
governments, federalist or sovereignist, subscribed. But on the
other, regionalist premiers who took strong anti-Ottawa
stands were potential allies for even the Parti Québécois
government. This second effect became particularly evident
when constitutional negotiations began to gather steam in the
late 1970s, and especially in the "patriation round" set in motion by Prime Minister Trudeau after the Quebec referendum

in May 1980. At a constitutional conference in the fall of that year, when Trudeau unveiled his centralist version of constitutional reform, Newfoundland Premier Brian Peckford said he preferred René Lévesque's vision of Canada to Trudeau's. Lévesque, Peckford, Lougheed and five other premiers formed a "Gang of Eight" to resist Trudeau's proposals.

The Gang of Eight adventure, of course, ended disastrously for Quebec at the Ottawa constitutional conference in November 1981. Much has been said and written about who double-crossed whom at that conference, but for our purposes here that is not the important question. What is important is that Quebec's differences with the federal government turned out to be of a different order from those of the other provinces. What were irreducible demands for Quebec were bargaining chips for the others. So in the end Quebec stood alone, just as it had when previous rounds of constitutional negotiation had come close to consummation in 1964 and 1971. But there was a difference this time: in contrast to those earlier occasions, the Pierre Trudeau of the early 1980s did not regard the Quebec government's opposition as sufficient reason not to go ahead with his constitutional project. Canada got its new constitution, without Quebec's signature and with a notwithstanding clause — which had the potential to vitiate Trudeau's beloved Charter of Rights and Freedoms — thrown in to placate the dissident premiers in English Canada.

From Antinationalism to Nationalism

It is generally considered that it was in the latter part of the Diefenbaker era that relations between Canada and the United States deteriorated to their lowest level in modern history. The temporary recall of our ambassador, Charles Ritchie, symbolizes this period. In early 1980, again under a Conservative administration, the atmosphere was so different that the United States was heaping lavish praise on Canada for Ambassador Ken Taylor's protection of six American diplomats during the hostage-taking in Iran and full-page "Thank you, Canada" ads were running in American newspapers. But within months, with the Trudeau Liberals back in power, relations between Canada and the U.S. went into a downward vortex that at one point had our external affairs minister, Mark

MacGuigan, wondering out loud whether our relations could ever be normalized, while others wondered what, in fact, "normal" was.

The 1980s began with increasing Canadian investment in the United States, including attempts at some buyouts and equity positions. In dollar amounts, Canadian investment in the United States equalled American investment in Canada. While there had been some reduction of American control in Canada since 1972, this in no sense represented a victory for Canadian economic nationalism. Rather, it meant that Canadian business had gained for itself a larger share of the continental economy.

Of more significance perhaps was the dream of the new American president, Ronald Reagan, of an American economic unit encompassing both Canada and Mexico. To conform with the north-south alignment, Canada would have to abandon its traditional — if increasingly tenuous — east-west ties.

Canada had always been willing to make a wide variety of political and economic concessions to the United States. Our destinies were linked; we were willing to be reliable suppliers of resources; through NORAD, the DEW line, and the Defence Production Sharing Agreements, we had political commitments, both contractual and unspoken. But the issue of control remained apart. And it was precisely this issue that was first on the agenda throughout the 1980s.

Matters were greatly complicated because control over energy and resources became an issue within Canada as well as in Canadian-American negotiations. While the U.S. considered energy and resources a continental matter, Ottawa and the various provinces argued about provincial versus federal jurisdiction over them. This confusion was evident as early as the 1960s with the Columbia River development. The Columbia twists from the Kootenays in British Columbia through Washington and Oregon to the Pacific. To harness the river to provide hydroelectricity to the power-starved Pacific Northwest, reservoirs had to be created in Canada. How Canada — or more precisely B.C. — was to be reimbursed involved a struggle between B.C. and the federal government. B.C. finally prevailed, but resolution of the struggle still left the basic conflict between provincial control of resources and overriding federal responsibility for international treaties and trade. The signing ceremony for the Columbia River project illustrated this unresolved conflict. President Lyndon Johnson and B.C. Premier W.A.C. Bennett were there, pen in hand and ready to sign; Prime Minister Pearson was also there pen in hand, but with nothing to sign.

The Columbia precedent set some of the parameters for the struggle between Alberta and Ottawa for control of gas and oil. The federal government's National Energy Program of 1980-81 was in part an attempt at an end run around the whole issue of provincial jurisdiction, but it was seen in Washington as a direct attack on secure American access to the continental resource, discrimination against American oil companies, and a blow against the sacred "marketplace." The fact that the Reagan government was correct on all these points in no way diminished the federal government's enthusiasm for the NEP. There was just too much at stake.

Throughout all the trade negotiations, the Americans had only one item on their agenda. This was secure access to energy and what has been described as "national treatment," which in the context of the relative size of our two economies means control and ownership of the continental resource. This we have consistently rejected. To the United States, the NEP was the codification, the setting in stone, of this rejection. In negotiations before and after the NEP, Canada was willing to make any other concessions to the U.S. Indeed there was no area of American annoyance with Canada that we would not negotiate. If the weak Foreign Investment Review Agency did manage to grow a tooth, we would extract it. There would be no more talk of a "son of NEP" national industrial strategy. The more amenable we became, the tougher the Americans got.

Thus the manifold reasons for the crisis in Canada-U.S. relations in the early 1980s boil down to the competing nationalisms of our two states. The victory of Ronald Reagan in 1980 meant the reassertion of a strident American nationalism throughout the world; getting the continent and thus the hemisphere to move in lockstep was the first essential priority. The reaffirmation of Canadian nationalism, if any policy directed by Pierre Trudeau could be considered nationalist, was inwardly directed. At its core, its aim was to strengthen the central government in a political sense vis-à-vis Quebec and to buttress this authority with economic clout. In the brave new world of oil and OPEC, Marc Lalonde and his bureaucrats found the fuel that would drive the Ottawa money mill and hence provide Quebec with what Robert Bourassa during another incarnation called "profitable federalism." Federal control over energy made Jean Chrétien plausible when he warned that an independent Quebec would not have access to cheap gas — all because Claude Morin and a few others wanted the prestige of driving around foreign capitals with Quebec flags on the hoods of their Cadillacs.

Political observers tend to agree that economic issues are the hinge on which elections swing. All politics turn on economic self-interest, or perceived economic self-interest. During the referendum campaign in Quebec, the federalist side unleashed a barrage of arguments that addressed Quebec's economic self-interest in a confederal arrangement with English-speaking Canada and buried the largely undefinable issues of dignity and self-governed national destiny on which the PQ campaign rested. In retrospect, some wistful Péquistes found it extraordinary that as many as 40 per cent of Quebecers resisted the weight of those economic arguments.

We have seen how André Laurendeau came to realize that the mandate of the Royal Commission on Bilingualism and Biculturalism to investigate English-French relations could only be pursued within the wider context of Canadian-American relations. By 1980 Trudeau had reluctantly come to a similar conclusion. Trudeau's often expressed fear of nationalist movements was that one knows where they begin but can have no idea of how they end. The same thing can be said of antinationalism. In Trudeau's case antinationalism worked its way around through about a three-quarter turn to a form of Canadian nationalism.

In terms of the item uppermost on his agenda, Trudeau had achieved impressive short-term success. The Quebec referendum had resulted in a victory not only for federalism but also for the Trudeau vision of Canada, as the 60 per cent No vote of May 1980 was followed by repatriation of the constitution with a charter of rights. By the time of Trudeau's retirement in early 1984, the Lévesque government was a shambles. Later that year, with Trudeau and his confrontational approach gone, Lévesque himself was saying that federalism was a "beau risque." Even the separatists had become federalists.

This victory appeared to overshadow other, less promising developments. The NEP, conceived and executed at a time of high oil prices, had been undercut not so much by the opposition of Alberta, the oil companies and the Americans as by the falling oil prices of the early eighties. The recession of 1981-83, from which the country was only beginning to recover, and the annual $35-billion budget deficits it ushered in seriously reduced the government's room to manoeuvre. A 1981 budget that might have alleviated the situation by closing some tax loopholes was undone by a business campaign reminiscent of the one that brought down Walter Gordon's budget in 1963. And militant nationalism continued to prevail in the United States, as Ronald Reagan sailed to easy reelection in 1984.

Thus, Trudeau left his successor, Brian Mulroney (leaving aside John Turner's brief term in office), an uneasy economic situation — particularly in terms of Canada's economic relations with the United States — but an apparently very promising constitutional one. This was especially so since one of the most divisive forces in the country, Trudeau himself, was now out of the picture, and the PQ government was headed for almost certain electoral defeat within a year. Mulroney led a federal government that, for the first time since the early Trudeau years, enjoyed broad support in both Quebec and English Canada. The time seemed propitious to right the most serious deficiency of the Trudeau constitutional legacy: encouraged by his close friend and adviser Lucien Bouchard, Mulroney promised to make it possible for Quebec to sign the Canadian constitution "with honour and enthusiasm."

5

The 1980s: The Corporate Decade

Between Pierre Elliott Trudeau's accession to office in 1968 and the "walk in the snow" on February 29, 1984 during which he decided that it was time to get out, there were major shifts in the underlying conditions under which leaders of the government of Canada, and indeed all governments, did their jobs. These shifts would continue to operate as Brian Mulroney tried to grapple with the formidable problems of the late 1980s. Perhaps the most significant shift was the steady growth of global economic activity that escaped the regulatory purview of any individual national government.

The Borderless World of the Multinationals

The most conspicuous manifestation of the new global economy was the multinational corporation. While it had always been common for a company to do business outside its country of origin, what had developed by the early 1970s was something quite different. As Richard J. Barnet and Ronald E. Müller wrote in their landmark 1974 study of the multinational corporation, *Global Reach*, the managers of these corporations "are the first to have developed a plausible model of the future that is global. They exploit the advantages of mobility while workers and governments are still tied to particular territories. For this reason, the corporate visionaries are far ahead of the rest of the world in making claims on the future. In making business decisions today they are creating a politics for the next generation."

A parallel development was the emergence of an international financial system based on stateless and regulation-free Eurodollars, a system that grew from $9 billion in 1964 to almost $1 trillion in 1980. The growth of the Eurodollar market helped bring down the Bretton Woods financial order in the early 1970s and was spurred on by the influx of oil billions later in the decade. The existence of a private, unregulated international financial system further weakened the capacity of national governments to manage their economies.

Different countries responded to these developments in different ways. Japan maintained the partnership between government and business that had helped make it the great economic success story of the 1960s and the 1970s. The government of France, Socialist after 1981, greatly expanded its presence in the economy, then pulled back in the face of the recession of the early 1980s. But the response most characteristic of the times was the one favoured by Britain and the United States. Instead of trying to challenge, circumvent or opt out of the economy's new imperviousness to regulation, Prime Minister Margaret Thatcher and President Ronald Reagan enthusiastically accepted it. So what if governments couldn't control the economy? In the view of Thatcher and Reagan — and a body of economic thought as old as Adam Smith — governments were best off keeping their noses out of the economy in any case.

The old forms of government intervention no longer seemed to work, no convincing alternative to the Thatcher-Reagan approach had yet been formulated, and the economic lot of some influential sectors of the population did improve in the 1980s (although the bills would later begin to fall due). As a result, the new conservatism enjoyed a virtual monopoly of political discourse, especially in the United States. Late in the decade, the Iran-Contra arms scandal, the revelation of the savings and loan scams in the United States and the slowing of economic growth would make the Conservative Revolution look a bit tattered, but the underlying developments that had given rise to it continued to operate.

Thus, in 1989 the *Wall Street Journal* cheerfully announced the return of the "one-worlders." These new one-worlders weren't the radical socialists of the old-time Marxist variety who envisaged the world as a single nation of workers. Rather, "They are economists and academics who believe that in a global economy ... the economic fortunes of individual countries aren't important any more .... Trade deficits and other statistics are only artificial figures in what has become a multinational corporate economy." In this new one world, American companies may manufacture their products in Japan, sell them in the United States, and repatriate much of the profit. These transactions will show up as part of the multibillion-dollar U.S. trade deficit with Japan, but in reality such a deficit is no more significant than one that Kansas may run with Montana.

The *Wall Street Journal* article reported that one of the main international exponents of this theory, Kenichi Ohmae, had surprised a Washington conference by saying that as long as U.S. multinationals were content to make products in Japan, the U.S. shouldn't care if fewer American goods are exported. National borders are disappearing; money is transmitted electronically; in fact everything moves with ease except labour. And Ohmae, warming to his Washington audience, claimed that American industry shouldn't even be concerned about the loss of jobs because many of the losses are among minority youth and "most of these guys don't vote." In more recent speeches and writings, Ohmae has developed this point to include the notion that labour assumes less and less importance as the labour content of manufacturing is reduced. Furthermore, during a 1990 visit to Canada, Ohmae stated that there was no such thing as a Canadian national interest.

In our account of the postwar period, we have emphasized the consistent tendency towards American-Canadian economic integration, which by the late 1980s would be virtually complete. Regional integration was also occurring in Europe and Asia over the same period. But integration did not stop at regional borders any more than at national ones. While "fortress America", "fortress Europe" and "fortress Asia" were being created, they were simultaneously penetrating, undermining and destroying one another. In his latest work, *The Borderless World*, Ohmae discusses the emergence of the interlinked economy (ILE) of the "Triad" (the U.S., Europe and Japan): "It has become so powerful that it has swallowed most consumers and corporations, made traditional national borders almost disappear, and pushed bureaucrats, politicians and the military towards the status of declining industries. For all practical purposes the ILE has made obsolete the traditional instruments of central bankers — interest rates and money supply."

In other words, the creation of the super trading blocs does not freeze the movement towards globalization. The true multinational is stateless in the sense that it will operate within the "new Europe" as it operates in Japan and in America. Ohmae argues — as do other economists, notably Robert Reich — that through joint ventures, international marketing agreements and equity investments the global economy is controlled by true international monopolies. Ohmae asks, for example, whether IBM in Japan is "an American or Japanese company":

> Its workforce of 20,000 is Japanese, but its equity holders are American. Even so, over the past decade IBM Japan has provided, on average, three times more tax revenue to the Japanese government than has Fujitsu. What is its nationality? Or what about Honda's operations in Ohio? Or Texas Instruments' memory-chip activities in Japan? Are they "American" products? If so, what about the cellular phones sold in Tokyo that contain components made in the United States by American workers who are employed by the U.S division of a Japanese company? Sony has facilities in Dothan, Ala., from which it sends audiotapes and video tapes to Europe. What is the nationality of these products or the operation that makes them?

All the American automobile manufacturers are involved in joint ventures with Japanese manufacturers in both marketing and production. GM and Suzuki manufacture jointly in Canada, as do Mazda and Ford in California. The changes to the economic landscape are especially dramatic in the United States, which is used to having its corporations operate abroad but less accustomed to having other countries' giants operate in its territory. While American corporations infiltrate the new Europe and range throughout the Pacific Rim, America becomes home to European cartels and the *keiretsu* of Japan. Direct foreign investment in the U.S. is minuscule in comparison to the size of the American economy, but it is growing rapidly. Today it is about the same dollar amount as American direct investment outside the U.S., with more than half of the total having been invested in the last decade. In 1987, of the then $262 billion in direct foreign investment in the United States, almost $165 billion had arrived since 1980. Most of this new investment has come from Japan, which by the early 1990s will succeed Britain as the largest foreign investor in the U.S. The British took more than two centuries to reach a level of investment in the United States that the Japanese will surpass in ten years.

But this is only the tip of the penetration of foreign capital into the United States. The transformation of the U.S. from the world's creditor to the world's major debtor is an old story by now. There is more than $1 trillion in private foreign holdings of U.S. securities. Dependent on Japanese and German bankers, the U.S. is severely restricted in both its monetary and fiscal policies. Proposals have been made that debt-ridden countries such as Mexico should get out from under their burdens by exchanging debt for equity. What would happen if the U.S. — or the second largest debtor country, Canada — should also became the victim of such a swap? What happens when there is nothing left to sell? What happens if western Europe finds a more attractive investment climate in, say, eastern Europe? Money that flows in can also flow out.

The "one world" argument raises some other thorny questions as well. If the nation-state is becoming economically — and therefore politically — irrelevant, who or what takes over its responsibilities? And how are these responsibilities paid for? These questions assume special importance in the United States and Canada when one looks at those countries' budget deficits and the methods governments use to bring them under control: social spending cutbacks and shifting the tax base to consumption taxes. It is only natural that if the nation-state is irrelevant to the new multinational corporation, neither it nor its owners should pay for its upkeep.

But perhaps the element that is most resistant to the calculations of the one-worlders is labour. Most experts agree that one of the early results of the Canada-U.S. Free Trade Agreement has been the transfer of blue-collar manufacturing jobs to the United States — primarily its low-wage areas. Yet overall, the deindustrialization of the United States continues apace, primarily a reflection of new technologies that erode the labour component in all manufacturing. Labour now accounts for less than one quarter of the cost of most manufactured products. But deindustrialization also reflects the movement of industries and the export of jobs. In Mexico, for example, GM has opened as many plants as it has shut down up north, and Japanese electronics firms are also extremely active.

If capital has no national interest any more, and if, as Kenichi Ohmae suggests, the only element in production that is not easily transported is labour, then it naturally follows that it will be labour that is most vitally concerned with its nation or community. And so while the *Wall Street Journal* gloats about the profitability of the new internationalism, those who oppose it or recognize themselves as its victims are left with the tired banners of nationalism and cast as modern Luddites. This marginalization affected the opposition both to the Canada-U.S. Free Trade Agreement and to the current initiative towards a free trade agreement with Mexico. For Canadians, the debate surrounding an agreement with Mexico initially focused on the question of whether Canada should join the discussions. In fact, however, whether Canada joins or not is immaterial. We will be included in whatever agreement is reached between Mexico and the U.S. Since we are in it — just as we are inexorably in the process of globalization as a whole — what can be made of it? What forms of international cooperation between peoples can be developed so that the industrialization of Mexico does not come at the expense of the people of Canada or the United States? What rights and what guarantees can be won?

As Robert Reich has noted, the real issue in the United States is the state versus its own multinationals. As the trend towards globalism is confirmed, this contradiction becomes more apparent and perhaps sharper. Thus in Europe, politicians no less backward than Margaret Thatcher (before her downfall) have concluded guarantees of labour rights within the grandiose plans for integration in 1992. In Canada, we seem blinded by the overwhelming presence, power and dominance of the United States, so that it is difficult for us to see that the American people are themselves being victimized in the globalization of the economy in the same manner, if not yet to the same degree, as Canadians and Mexicans. It has become clear that no effective challenge to the economic dominance of the multinationals and the ideological hegemony of the right will be mounted by waging rearguard actions against the new "one world." A more promising avenue may be to concentrate on establishing different conditions under which it will be brought about.

Brian Mulroney: Pragmatic Conservative

When Brian Mulroney's Conservatives swept to power in September 1984, there were many who interpreted their election victory as meaning that the Reagan-Thatcher approach to government had spread to Canada. After all, the interventionist Liberals had been decisively rejected, like the British Labour Party and the Democrats in the United States before them. And there were certainly plenty of people in the new Tory caucus, some of them in positions of considerable influence, who talked like the people who surrounded Reagan and Thatcher.

And yet, the man who headed the new government was fundamentally a pragmatist. In his brief term as opposition leader, he had supported the Trudeau government's reaffirmation of official bilingualism and its initiative against extra-billing by doctors, thus evading its attempts to box him into a right-wing corner. His election victory had more or less fallen into his lap as the Liberals self-destructed, so that he had said little during the campaign that would pin him down to an ideological position of any sort.

According to conventional wisdom, Conservative leaders may play to right-wing sentiments in their own party and caucus, but to win elections and govern effectively they have to accept the political culture of the country. In referring to social programs as a "sacred trust," Mulroney had explicitly accepted this position, following in the tradition of pragmatic Tory leaders from John A. Macdonald to Joe Clark. In office, and especially after being reelected in 1988, he would move further and further away from that tradition, not so much because of his own inclinations as because changing circumstances made the conventional wisdom obsolete. Both Mulroney's centrist stance in 1984 and his eventual repudiation of it had much to do with the way in which he had become leader of the Conservative Party.

There is a deep, ongoing division in the Conservative Party that does not resolve itself by the disaffection of a faction or a split, as divisions do in most parties, but is rather contained in an awkward alliance that occasionally dissolves into a bitter leadership race. The rivals are variously termed "Red Tories," "Pink Tories" or "pragmatists" on one side and "right-wingers," "ideologues" or "true believers" on the other. The leadership triumphs of Robert Stanfield in 1967 and Joe Clark in 1976 were both victories for the "pragmatists." But in 1976, although the majority gave their votes to the "pragmatists," from the rhetoric of the campaign and the convention itself they clearly gave their hearts to the "ideologues."

Joe Clark's election victory in 1979 was, in fact, his defeat. His minority government was unable to function because of the ideological disputes within the cabinet. While Treasury Board President Sinclair Stevens operated from a position of "If it moves, privatize it," Minister of Energy Ray Hnatyshyn read the polls and wasn't sure selling off Petro-Canada was such a good idea. Even if the government's short life span did not give it time to do much more than retreat from the lottery field in the name of Clark's notion of Canada as a "community of communities," there were some within it who were intent on repealing every federal power gained since the outbreak of the Second World War. In *Discipline of Power*, Jeffrey Simpson vividly describes the policy pratfalls of the Clark government. Making every allowance for bad luck, inexperience and the government's astonishing inability to distinguish a minority from a majority, the factional split within the party played its role in bringing the government down and in the desperate years that followed put the Tories on the political margin through the Quebec referendum and the constitutional debate.

The Logical Prime Minister

There is a story of a friend of Winston Churchill's comforting the old warrior after his postwar election defeat: "It's a blessing in disguise." "If it is," Churchill answered, "it is disguised very well."

Brian Mulroney could have thought his defeat at the 1976 leadership convention an equally well-disguised blessing. Nevertheless, that is what it was. It gave him a chance to reinvent himself in terms of the split within the party. His job at the Iron Ore Company of Canada, a Canadian subsidiary of Cleveland-based Hanna Mining, gave him an entrée to where the real continental power lay and an unparalleled education in the relationship between economic power and politics. As a boy, he had once confided that his ambitions lay in politics, not business, because the power was in politics. He learned at IOC that the relationship is not as simple or as onesided as that. His main function at IOC was public relations and he honed his skills superbly. Even when head office decided to close down Schefferville in 1982, Mulroney was capable of turning it into an acceptable corporate decision and a personal triumph. These factors, combined with his still underestimated political skills, his rock-hard determination to win and his status as a Quebecer *pure laine* in the new political geography of Canada, made him the logical prime minister — at least in his own mind.

When he ran for the leadership in 1976, Brian Mulroney was relatively unknown outside of Quebec, but he was very well known inside the Progressive Conservative Party. He was identified firmly (but not solely) with the Dalton Camp anti-Diefenbaker faction, and his friends were young Tories like Roy McMurtry in Ontario. During the campaign to succeed John Diefenbaker, Mulroney, still in his twenties, was a key leader of Davie Fulton's campaign and played an important role in eventually moving Fulton to Robert Stanfield. Flora MacDonald, one of Stanfield's main people, described young Mulroney and his friend Lowell Murray as "our sort of group.... They're our kind of guys. They're progressives."

A still worse sin in the eyes of the Tory right was that Mulroney had too many Quebec Liberal friends — and some acquaintances who were even more dubious. He was a protégé of Judge Robert Cliche, a former Quebec NDP leader. Robert Bourassa was an influential friend, and his campaign was lavishly financed by Paul Desmarais, also closely associated with the Liberal French Power strategy.

Mulroney could not understand the criticism he received on this account. In Quebec at that time a politician without Liberal friends was one with no friends at all. But when he arrived at the 1976 convention in Ottawa, he was the candidate everyone turned out to hate. Even though he knew he was beaten when John Diefenbaker went out of his way to disqualify him for leader because he had no parliamentary experience (a thought that was silly even then), he still didn't seem to know why. Surrounded by the rising right-wing rhetoric, he gave a bland speech and was relatively gentle with the favourite Tory targets, Pierre Trudeau and the CBC.

Brian Mulroney's weaknesses in 1976 were not only in the friends he had but also in the politics he apparently didn't have. Seven years later these weaknesses became his strength.

Attack from the Right

As the disastrous (for Joe Clark and the Tories) 1980 election campaign drew to a close, the reemerging Pierre Trudeau began to scatter lines of poetry into his speeches. On one occasion he paraphrased Yeats:

> Things fall apart; the centre cannot hold
> And mere anarchy is loosed upon the Tory Party.

The pressure on Clark came from several sources. While most of the public expressions revolved around his image of weakness and incompetence, the real concerted effort to remove him came from the ideological right wing of the party.

A Conservative convention in 1981 almost broke up in chaos as delegates from the floor demanded changes in resolutions presented by the leadership. Speakers were loudly applauded for demanding that the Canada Pension Plan be dismantled. Others demanded clearcut positions on capital punishment and abortion. Ronald Reagan and Margaret Thatcher were the ascendant stars, and Joe Clark was the wimp. At a conference in 1982, Sinclair Stevens sensed a weakening of the position on privatizing all crown corporations. "I am stunned ... to hear this soft attitude to state ownership," he shouted. "It's pure socialism."

The demand for the Conservative Party to shift to the right and distinguish itself from the Liberals was pushed not only by party activists but also by powerful voices in the so-called business community. "The only real difference between existing political parties is the pace with which they are leading us to socialism," concluded one business publication in 1982.

That same year, acerbic political commentator Allan Fotheringham wrote a column on the results of a survey of delegates to the 1981 Tory convention. The survey showed, according to Fotheringham, that the typical delegate was "against most of the advances of mankind since the children were released from the mines." By large majorities, the delegates revealed that they were antimetric, antibilingual, antiwelfare. Almost all favoured a large reduction in government social spending, especially unemployment insurance, family allowances and job creation programs. Months later, columnist Richard Gwyn commented on the same survey in the context of the early stages of the renewed leadership race in the party. Gwyn expanded on the ideological struggle underlying the contest just beginning: "The rightwingers are about to provoke the first real debate about the nature of Canada's political system since the formation of the New Democratic Party in 1959."

Not if Brian Mulroney could have anything to say about it.

The Politics of Deal-Making

Brian Mulroney's early underground campaign for the leadership in 1983 consisted of bland speeches to corporate audiences, especially in the "oil patch." Here he likened the National Energy Program to a late-night gas station holdup and promised that the days of Marc Lalonde and his socialist cohorts were over — all fairly standard stuff for the times. For the most part, his speeches were crafted to express, or at least to imply, support for every side of every question.

He also dined out with most of the dissidents in the federal caucus. What was discussed or promised is not on the record, but when the crunch came at the 1983 convention, those members of the caucus who belonged to what Dalton Camp once called the "cashew coalition" shared the stage with Mulroney.

Mulroney's two policy announcements leading up to the 1983 convention — his opposition to free trade and his hard line on Quebec (in power he would firmly contradict both) — did not cut much ice anywhere. Wasn't he, after all, the candidate who cared so little for policy that he scribbled his policy on French-English relations on the white bag provided on a Quebecair flight? And didn't he, while opposing free trade, also promise to eliminate any and every irritant in Canada-U.S. relations? Every other issue was condensed to winning an election.

It was Brian Mulroney's studied indifference to all the policy debates wracking the party that made him the logical solution to the impasse. This indifference was, of course, not only deliberate on Mulroney's part but the essence of his strategy. Thus, to say that Brian Mulroney is unprincipled is true, but it is not the whole truth. It would be more precise to say that it is against Brian Mulroney's principles to have principles.

This is perhaps the one unifying thread in Mulroney's approach to politics. It comes, at least in part, from his background as a labour negotiator, and it consists in valuing the act of signing a deal above what is actually in the deal. This approach has both its advantages and its dangers.

Once in office, Mulroney saw the prime minister as a power broker; his function was to make deals with other power brokers in whatever area happened to be in the forefront at the time. In the case of the constitution, for example, the other power brokers were the provincial premiers, and he saw the Meech Lake Accord as a good deal not because of its intrinsic merits but because it was acceptable to all the premiers. If a much more centralist (or much more decentralist) constitution had been acceptable to them, then that too would have been acceptable to Mulroney.

This approach was in direct contrast to that of Pierre Trudeau, who cared about what was in the constitution considerably more than about who signed it. He was quite prepared to repatriate the constitution with the support of only two provinces if necessary; indeed, he would have happily repatriated it with the support of no provinces had the situation arisen. This is not to say that Trudeau's approach was right and Mulroney's wrong. Trudeau's approach led to fifteen years of confrontation and bitterness. But being conciliatory does not, in itself, solve the problem. The question is: towards whom is one being conciliatory? In other words, who is in on the decision?

In the case of the constitution, Mulroney himself indicated that everyone had to be in on it because it is more than a "piece of paper." But "everyone" simply meant all the premiers; it did not mean there has to be democratic decision-making or broad consultation within each province. This, however, was precisely the problem with Meech Lake and one of the main reasons for its demise: few people outside French Quebec were committed to it because they had not been not brought in on the decision. Understanding Mulroney's approach to politics also helps clarify his relationship to the right-wing agenda that would be carried out in his name. It was not his agenda — any more than any other agenda would have been — but his ability to make deals, and his lack of concern about what was in those deals, made him highly desirable as a front person.

If Mulroney's approach differed from Trudeau's, it nevertheless has a long history in Canada; Mackenzie King and Sir John A. Macdonald were master practitioners of this form of politics. If Mulroney did not meet with the same success as these masters, it was not because he was not a match for them in craft and guile, but because he was governing a different kind of country. And it was different in large part because of the evolution of Quebec, which took a new turn after 1980.

Quebec's Distinct Capitalism

As we have seen, economic arguments were central to the victory of the No campaign in the Quebec referendum of 1980. A decade later, with Quebec nationalism again on the rise, those arguments had considerably less resonance. This change was partly the result of the weakening of the Canadian federal structure that came about with growing globalization and especially with the Canada-U.S. Free Trade Agreement and partly the result of the emergence of a new Francophone Quebec business elite and the newly positive relationship that the elite had with the Quebec government and public opinion.

Like most of North America, Quebec entered the 1980s on a note of economic distress and was plagued by shutdowns and layoffs, not least in its export-oriented forestry and mining sectors. Unemployment remained near 14 per cent through 1982 and 1983 and averaged just below 13 per cent in the "recovery" year of 1984. One region that suffered more visibly than most was the North Shore of the Gulf of St. Lawrence, where several major employers cut their activities drastically. Among them was the Iron Ore Company of Canada, which closed its concentrator and pelletizing plant in Sept-Îles in 1981 and its Schefferville mining operation in 1982. There a committee of the Quebec National Assembly met in the town's high school gymnasium to discuss the plight of the community. The star witness was the president of IOC, Brian Mulroney, in his last act before returning to his first love, politics. With the closing of the mine, Schefferville's population was reduced to a fraction of its former size.

Elsewhere in Quebec, however, the seeds were planted for a very different turn of economic events. In the Beauce, long viewed as a sleepy, old-fashioned corner of Quebec tucked into a remote area along the border with Maine (and once noted as the source of more than half the world's commercial maple syrup production), local traditions of community solidarity and hard work had turned cottage industries into thriving businesses. While most of these have remained small, a few have grown to multinational scope. The Beauce not only gave the world Vachon cakes and Dionne textiles but also spawned Canam Manac Group Inc., built by entrepreneur Marcel Dutil into one of the continent's top makers of steel joists for the construction industry. The company got its start selling to the New England market; its palindromic name is taken from a contraction of Canadian-American spelled forward and then backward.

Despite its often low wage levels, the Beauce began to achieve a modest prosperity, and a number of newspaper and magazine articles in the late 1970s called attention to the phenomenon of this poor, self-reliant farming area suddenly bursting with a wide array of industries with only scant help from outside investors. It was a phenomenon that would grip Quebec as a whole in the 1980s as modern capitalism, often viewed in the past with deep suspicion, achieved a respectability and acceptance that it had gained long before in most of North America. In yet another respect Quebec was moving into the North American mainstream, but at its own pace and in its own distinct fashion.

The early days of the Quiet Revolution had been marked by a proliferation of *sociétés d'état*, or state corporations (as government-owned corporations are called in antimonarchist Quebec). None came anywhere close in size or prestige to Hydro-Quebec, but they spread their tentacles into various sectors of the economy — including Sidbec in steel, Rexfor in forestry, Soquem in mining, Soquip in oil exploration, Soquia in food processing, Société Nationale de l'Amiante in asbestos, and the Société Générale de Financement, a general investment fund. Besides the state corporations, the government also established the Caisse de Dépôt et Placement du Québec, a financially powerful administrator of tens of billions of dollars in public pension funds with significant holdings in many publicly traded companies. The state corporations, notably Hydro itself, as well as the Caisse de Dépôt, were created largely with the aim of giving French-speaking Quebecers some of the levers of economic control that had eluded them in the private sector.

Soon after the Parti Québécois took power in 1976, indeed partly by default with outside investment dwindling, small locally owned businesses began to play a more important role in the Quebec economy. Little noticed during the years of tumult, significant change had occurred in the way many people perceived their economic destinies. Educational reforms begun in the early 1960s had created great leaps in both the number and the qualifications of university graduates. At first, many of these graduates got jobs in the expanding state corporations. Hiring at these corporations slowed down in the 1970s, but at the same time the dominant Anglo-run firms became less reticent about hiring and promoting Francophones. And the doors to the private sector were opened wider by the emergence and growth of a rising core of Francophonerun firms.

Bombardier Inc. is often cited as a shining example of a Quebec firm that went from humble origins to break into the corporate big leagues. It is also an example of how government promotion of economic nationalism can sometimes pay off. In 1973 the low bid for an order of subway cars for the Montreal metro came from British-controlled Canadian Vickers, which had won a previous contract ten years earlier. But the Liberal government of Robert Bourassa gave the nod instead to Bombardier, which badly needed to diversify beyond its faltering snowmobile business. The ostensible reason for awarding the contract to Bombardier related to design technicalities, but it was plain to nearly everyone that government industrial strategy had more to do with the decision. The thinking in government circles was that foreign-owned Vickers would treat the order as a one-off deal while home-grown Bombardier would use it as a springboard to build an aggressive, export-oriented business in rail and transit equipment. On this occasion at least, the government's thinking proved farsighted and accurate.

Bombardier has not always had things its own way. In 1977 the avowedly nationalist Lévesque government chose General Motors over Bombardier to build buses for Quebec's urban transit systems. Lévesque was under pressure at the time to show the Americans that he wasn't a northern version of Fidel Castro; what better way to do this than to do a favour for GM? But Bombardier's best friends turned out to be the avowedly noninterventionist Mulroney Tories, from whom it bought the federally owned aircraft maker Canadair in 1986 for the bargain price of $120 million (Canadair's land holdings alone were worth more than that). A few months later, Ottawa awarded Bombardier a juicy contract for the maintenance of CF-18 military aircraft despite a lower and technically superior bid from Winnipeg-based (but foreign-owned) Bristol Aerospace. But if the CF-18 contract was advantageous to Bombardier, it would prove politically costly to Mulroney and to all who sought a peaceful settlement of Quebec's differences with the Canadian constitution: in the west, and especially in Manitoba, it would help fuel the resentment of central Canada in general and Quebec in particular that would play such a large role in bringing down the Meech Lake Accord.

Bombardier is still the biggest and best-known of Quebec's Francophone-run multinational industrial companies, but it is not alone in that category. Though few companies have seen government largesse on the same grand scale, hundreds of smaller firms in virtually every area of economic endeavour were able to finance their growth with the help of something known in English as Quebec Stock Savings Plans. The QSSP program was introduced in 1979 by Jacques Parizeau, then finance minister in the Lévesque government, and was confirmed by the probusiness Bourassa Liberals after they defeated the PQ in 1985. Parizeau, one of the architects of the Quiet Revolution, had been vilified by business people for his high-tax, high-deficit budgets, but he proved he could be flexible. QSSPs provided generous tax writeoffs to purchasers of eligible shares in Quebec-based companies. Besides helping such firms raise capital, the program defused some complaints about high taxation and whetted the appetites of people who had never before played the stock market. By the late 1980s, 14 per cent of Quebec adults were shareholders in publicly traded companies, still slightly below the Canadian average but well above the 5 per cent who had been shareholders a decade earlier.

The QSSP program really came into its own in 1983 when Parizeau changed the rules, reducing the incentives for investments in blue-chip stocks but raising the writeoffs available on shares in smaller, riskier companies. A deep recession was ending, many small and medium-sized companies were being listed on the stock exchange for the first time, and the money came pouring in. Most of these shares, though, were severely hurt in the October 1987 stock market crash, and the ardour of many small investors was crushed. This knocked the wind out of QSSPs, and few eligible issues were offered in the following years.

The PQ's first term in office had been marked by cool relations with business, but in Quebec, as in so many other places during the 1980s, the government started learning to get along better with the corporate sector. This was made easier by the fact that a growing proportion of the faces in this sector belonged to Francophones. Big business no longer seemed so alien. Far from remaining objects of suspicion, homegrown millionaires who had made it into the big leagues were, for a brief period, cheered on and venerated by a sizable portion of the public, almost like star athletes. Even the crime-and-sports tabloid *Le Journal de Montréal* began carrying stock tables. In keeping with the spirit of the times, the depositor-owned Desjardins credit union movement began straying from its populist roots to move into corporate finance, and the once radical Quebec Federation of Labour established its own risk capital fund in 1984 with the stated goal of helping finance job creation but also with the aim of providing a healthy return on investment.

When the Liberals returned to power in 1985 after nine years in the political wilderness, they found the economic policies put in place in the PQ's second term much to their liking. One thing they did set about doing was to dismantle some of the government's holdings in the economy, as was happening in other parts of the world. The money-losing airline Quebecair was privatized, leading to heavy layoffs, and a state-owned sugar-beet refinery was sold to private owners and almost immediately shut down. Other privatizations stirred less controversy, covering assets that included paper mills, salt mines, fish processing plants and a pipe factory.

Even after these asset sales, the Quebec government retained a sizable and varied portfolio of industrial holdings. A Liberal Party position paper presented soon after the Liberals regained power argued that Quebec's new business dynamism made government involvement in the economy harder to justify and that the onus should be on the state to prove the need for public intervention. But this same paper argued that "privatization is not an end in itself. When it is required, privatization of a state corporation must seek to strengthen the economic structure of Quebec while assuring Quebec's presence in key economic sectors." Even in the age of Thatcher and Reagan, a society that fears for its cultural survival is less likely to give up what it sees as valuable collective tools.

Among the untouchable parts of this structure (along with the Caisse de Dépôt) was Hydro-Quebec. Robert Bourassa never lost his enthusiasm for exploiting the economic potential of Quebec's northern rivers, and just before he regained the premiership, his 1985 book *Power from the North* once again brought hydroelectricity and power exports to the centre of Quebec political debate. Bourassa proposed that Quebec dam the remaining rivers flowing into James Bay as well as a number of rivers on the North Shore for the sole purpose of exporting the power to the United States. The billions of dollars required for these gigantic projects would also come from the United States on the basis of firm contracts to purchase the power. Bourassa launched the book with a press conference in Washington and then announced his candidacy in a provincial byelection, campaigning with the book as his chief prop. The PQ retaliated with a book of its own, criticizing the feasibility of Bourassa's proposals — but not, of course, the principle of power exports.

Hydro-Quebec was not without its problems. While it concentrated on expanding its productive capacity, it had neglected vital maintenance on its distribution network, leading to a series of Quebec-wide blackouts in 1988 and 1989 as well as tens of thousands of localized power failures. And while Hydro's operating profits, projected to climb above $3 billion annually heading into the 1990s, looked impressive, the utility also faced staggering interest payments, which ate up close to 80 per cent of those operating profits. With its voracious appetite for fresh loans, Hydro-Quebec had long outgrown even the U.S. capital markets and was looking overseas for an increasing share of its borrowing requirements. Undeterred, Bourassa continued to flaunt Hydro-Quebec as a motor of economic growth, not only for the construction jobs it would create but also for its role in luring energy-hungry aluminum smelters and other heavy industry.

By 1988 Hydro had signed a series of new export contracts with power authorities in New York and New England that would run for up to thirty years and would involve annual sales of up to 14.6 billion kilowatthours of electricity. However, the Central Maine Power Company, which had agreed to purchase a total of 40 billion kilowatthours over a period of twenty-eight years beginning in 1992, cancelled its commitment in 1989 under pressure from environmentalists, who feared the damage transmission lines might cause and argued that Maine could use conservation measures to make up for its projected shortfall in electricity production. Meanwhile, the northern Quebec Cree began preparing a legal case aimed at halting the ambitious second phase of the James Bay project, which would flood vast areas of land and reshape a territory the size of France. They allege that the plans as laid out violate environmental assurances contained in the original agreement they negotiated with the government in the 1970s. Emboldened by the Maine decision, the Cree have cultivated the support of environmentalists in other states where utilities have signed contracts with Hydro-Quebec. With its elements of environmental concern, native rights and transborder alliances — and with the government of Canada, at least so far, standing on the sidelines — James Bay II may epitomize the emerging politics of the 1990s.

The growth of electricity exports was just one part of a tendency towards closer north-south economic ties. Several Quebec entrepreneurs have stated (with some justice) that they are made to feel more welcome in the United States than in Ontario, but Ontario business interests have also run up against obstacles in Quebec. In 1989 a Toronto-based consortium made a vigorous series of offers for the shares of the Montreal-based Steinberg Inc., a supermarket and real estate empire. But the Quebec government made it clear it wished to see control of Steinberg remain within Quebec, and the Caisse de Dépôt countered with a proposal of its own in partnership with a Montreal entrepreneur named Michel Gaucher. Owners of the family trust that controlled a majority of the voting shares found themselves under intense pressure to accept the Quebec offer, and the Ontario group was thwarted.

At about the same time, Paul Desmarais, chairman of the Montreal-based holding company Power Corp. of Canada and the controlling shareholder in pulp and paper giant Consolidated Bathurst, also of Montreal, wanted to take over rival papermaker Domtar, in which the Société Générale de Financement and the Caisse de Dépôt held large blocks of shares. But the government did not encourage the SGF and the Caisse to go along, and Desmarais dropped his proposal. Instead, he agreed to sell Consolidated Bathurst to Chicago-based Stone Container Corp., and neither Quebec nor Ottawa raised a finger to stop the sale.

The different treatment of the two cases hinged on more than just the fact that one outside bidder was from Ontario and the other from the United States. But it did send a confused set of signals. Some financial writers in Toronto have taken to using the sobriquet Quebec Inc. in allusion to the government's strategic cooperation with business. Government promotion of corporate interests can scarcely be viewed as a new phenomenon in North America, but in Quebec it has taken a somewhat different form. Putting Michel Gaucher in charge of Steinberg did not set a precedent; the Caisse had previously manoeuvred to enable New Brunswick-born financier Bertin Nadeau to take control of rival retailer Provigo.

Outside parallels with this distinctive form of public sector encouragement of individual business interests do not leap immediately to mind. More than anything, it is part of an exercise in building new structures of Francophone corporate control, but it has little in common with the legendary Japan Inc. approach to industrial growth, with the lockstep conjunction between public and private sectors that in the past enabled Japan to build overwhelming national strength in selected industries in preparation for its carefully coordinated assaults on foreign markets. Quebec Inc. is a very different world and still a rather small one. Most of the people in its inner orbits are on a first-name basis, and because there are so few of them, the same names crop up continually. This helps create a greater image of coordination than actually exists.

Despite the relentless rise of French-speaking business, a glance at the rankings of Quebec-based industrial companies shows that only a handful of the largest corporations are under French Canadian control. Of the twenty biggest private-sector employers in Quebec in 1988, as ranked by the weekly business newspaper *Les Affaires*, only six could be described as mostly under Francophone control. But as one goes further down the list, the proportion of French names increases; this gives a clearer idea of what has been happening in the Quebec economy, whose growth in the 1980s was driven by its plethora of small and medium-sized firms, many of them only a few years old.

University enrolments tell a similar story, one that would have been unimaginable a generation ago. Quebec in the late 1980s had only a quarter of Canada's population and slightly more than a fifth of its university students, yet it accounted for nearly half of Canadian students enrolled in business courses.

Most of these business students are Francophones, and they are likely to stay in Quebec. Thus, Quebec is going to have many more business people in the years to come, and this is bound to have its political and cultural consequences in the form of greater business influence over public policy and a more business-oriented general outlook among Quebecers.

The federal election of 1988 represented an early indication of those consequences. With its enthusiasm for business in general and north-south business ties in particular, Quebec warmly endorsed the Free Trade Agreement, and not only secured the Tory majority in the House of Commons but also became the only province to give the Tories more seats than in 1984. The new capitalist Quebec thus played a crucial role in bringing Canada into the era of free trade and in creating the conditions under which the major issues facing Canada after 1988 would be played out.

6

In the Wake of the Free Trade Agreement

Authors Stephen Clarkson and Christina McCall have suggested that the Canada-U.S. Free Trade Agreement is Canada's real constitution. They may be overstating matters, but there is no doubt that the FTA drastically altered the atmosphere in which any Canadian constitution can be conceived. Indeed, since a constitution presupposes the existence of a political entity, the FTA placed the whole exercise in question. Moreover, if we widen our consideration of the FTA to include the underlying principle on which the agreement rests — the primacy of the bottom line and the sanctity of economic competition — a country such as Canada that never made much economic sense now makes no sense at all.

Canada's Hobbled Economy
Canada has always represented the (perhaps temporary) triumph of the political imagination over cold economic reality. The formation of an alternative North American market and the subsequent decisions to maintain, protect and expand it, from the National Policy to the National Energy Program, were justified by political considerations, never economic ones. They represented an attempt to create an economic foundation for a political structure that otherwise would be dangerously weak.

However, that economic foundation has been eroding for some time. One indication of this erosion is the decline in east-west trade between the regions of Canada in favour of increased trade north-south. This shift is most pronounced in

Quebec-Ontario economic relations, which were the fulcrum of Confederation. Even before free trade, Ontario-Quebec trade was rapidly diminishing. In 1967, 13 per cent of Ontario's manufacturing shipments went to Quebec. By 1984, just as the free trade talks were beginning, this trade had already dropped to 8 per cent. In the same year 9 per cent of Ontario's manufacturing output was sold to other provinces. In 1984, therefore, the Canadian market for Ontario manufacturing output was less than 20 per cent of the total — considerably less than the U.S. market, which accounted for 30 per cent of Ontario's manufactured goods. (Ontario was somewhat more important to the Quebec economy, representing about 17 per cent of Quebec's manufacturing shipments.) With the FTA and the 1990 recession (according to the Canadian Labour Congress, whose estimates have proven to be the most reliable, more than 100,000 manufacturing jobs have been lost to free trade), there have been further declines in interprovincial shipments because the manufacturing sectors most heavily involved in interprovincial trade, such as textiles and furniture, have been the hardest hit. The plain and simple fact is that Canadians do not trade much with each other any more, and will do so less and less in the future.

However, the southern Ontario industrial heartland has always tried to keep some kind of coherence and integrity to the Canadian market. For example, the intricate system of equalization payments in which billions from Ontario (along with smaller amounts form Alberta and British Columbia) flowed through the federal government to the "have-not" provinces have never been opposed — mainly because all this money could be expected to flow back to Ontario in the form of payments for automobiles, electric appliances and all other forms of manufacture. As this assured market evaporates under free trade, one can be sure the enthusiasm for the continuance of these transfer payments will abate.

It is not so much that the Ontario industrialists have changed their ideology — that they have turned their backs on Canada for the gold of the U.S., as George Grant charged in the 1960s — as that these industrialists don't really exist any more. Our manufacturing sector has been almost totally alienated, as the saga of Buffalo-bound Varity, formerly Massey-

Ferguson, illustrates. If one forgets for a moment the unfortunate Robert Campeau and his dreams of expansion into the consumer marketplace, the big Canadian money is in resources, a sector that is almost totally dependent on the United States, and real estate, where with all due respect to Toronto's "world-class" pretensions the action has also been mainly in the U.S. Declining value of American real estate holdings is at the core of the Toronto Bronfman onion that is now unpeeling, and while the Reichmanns' most conspicuous troubles have been in London, they too have been hurt in the American real estate swamp.

Canada's financial dealings with the rest of the world also testify to its declining control over its own economic destiny. Canada's foreign debt now approaches $250 billion. We are second only to the United States and owe more than twice as much as the third most prolific debtor. Another measure of the extent of our problem is a comparison with Poland, considered an international economic basket case. Poland — with a population larger than Canada's — carries a foreign debt of $40 billion. Our foreign debt hobbles the Canadian economy and increasingly erodes the extent to which economic decision-making rests within Canada. For example, the high-interest, high-dollar policies of John Crow and the Bank of Canada have come under attack as creating the first "made in Canada recession." This charge is a seriously inflated estimate of the power Canada has over its own economy. We are competing for foreign money to roll over our current debt and finance new shortfalls. As the conditions worsen within our economy, the price for foreign money increases. And there is nothing we can do about it.

Thus, the New York office of the Deutsche Bank sent an advisory to institutional investors in the summer of 1990 complaining about the Canadian situation. "Besides the economic and fiscal deterioration, there is growing concern on the ability of government in general to govern," the advisory said as it listed recent political events in the peaceable kingdom. In this respect a debtor country is placed in a no-win situation. It needs foreign money to finance its debt, but to attract foreign money it must keep interest rates high even as the economy weakens, thus accentuating the "economic and fiscal deterioration." Not only is our recession not "made in Canada"; our monetary policy isn't either, since it responds essentially to the demands of international money markets. And neither, for that matter, is our central bank governor, John Crow, who apart from having been born in England and educated at Oxford, worked at the International Monetary Fund in Washington for a number of years before making a sideways career move to the Bank of Canada. Crow's career illustrates the way central banks often have closer links with one another and with international financial institutions than with the countries in which they operate.

While high interest rates bedevil the Mulroney government's attempts to reduce the deficit, the high Canadian dollar negates many of the benefits exporters hoped for under free trade. Thus, Serge Racine, head of Shermag, a Sherbrooke-based furniture maker with factories on both sides of the border, initially shared the enthusiasm of Quebec's ambitious and self-assured new business elite for the Free Trade Agreement. However, the sharp rise in the exchange rate of the Canadian dollar in 1988 and 1989 more than wiped out the benefit he had hoped to achieve from the lowering of U.S. tariff barriers, and to compensate he found himself importing components from the U.S. equal in value to the furniture he was exporting. Although not a believer in conspiracy theories, Racine said he was almost inclined to suspect that Canadian negotiators had secretly agreed to induce the Canadian currency to rise to make the agreement more palatable to Americans who feared Canadian competition. Many Canadians share his suspicion even if no smoking gun has been found.

According to the current rules, the game of global economic competition is increasingly difficult for Canada to play. With little to offer in the way of manufactured goods, especially in comparison with the rising economic powers of the Pacific Rim, our only real assets are natural resources and proximity to the United States. This is why the question of control of resources loomed so large in the negotiations leading to the Free Trade Agreement. From C.D. Howe to Pierre Trudeau, control over resources and energy was recognized as the essence of Canadian economic sovereignty. It was this that the FTA finally denied us. As Eric Kierans said during his testimony on the FTA, "What [the Americans] want is access to every bit of our land and resources. That is clear and what the agreement turned out to be. Anybody in the United States could have told you that this is what they would hold to. The rest of it was just filler material."

Changes in world economic patterns affect Canada, and we are not immune to the pressures these changes dictate. The deep structural changes in the Canadian economy also determine how the "national unity" game is played and what its outcome will be. In post-free trade Canada, it is much more difficult to sustain a convincing argument that Quebec's economic interests lie with English-speaking Canada. And it is at least as difficult to imagine what economic interests in English-speaking Canada would be advanced or salvaged by Quebec's remaining in Confederation. Industry in Ontario and Quebec alike is looking south, not east or west.

One indication of the new reality was a feeble premiers' conference in August 1990, at which Quebec was not represented. The conference reached an agreement to work towards dropping trade barriers between the provinces. Nobody paid much attention, because it just doesn't matter any more. If there is nothing more to Canada than the market that was created at the end of the nineteenth century, than there will be nothing left of it as the market disintegrates at the end of the twentieth century.

Region North America

The Canada-U.S. Free Trade Agreement came into effect in the final weeks of Ronald Reagan's presidency, and it included only one of the two partners Reagan had originally envisaged. Campaigning for office back in 1980, with fresh memories of the 1979 world oil shock and the long queues at gas stations in the U.S., candidate Reagan suggested that a North American free trade zone would suit United States interests quite handsomely by allowing free access to the abundant energy resources of Canada and Mexico. It hardly seemed to matter to Reagan that neither of his country's neighbours was especially interested in a scheme that failed to take their concerns into account. Canada, in fact, was in the process of adopting a National Energy Program aimed at increasing Canadian control of the oil industry, while Mexico, as a sizable oil exporter, was finding higher world prices quite to its liking and could see no real value in making it easier for the U.S. to plunder its resources.

Shortly after Reagan made the proposal, then-Prime Minister Trudeau and President José López Portillo disclaimed any interest in a trilateral trade deal. By the time Reagan became president, it even appeared that the new administration was walking away from the idea. The speechwriter who put the original words in Reagan's mouth began to play down the whole notion. The idea of a continental trade pact, or Region North America as it was called in stark Orwellian terms, was quietly put aside, but it was not laid to rest. The battles to win Canadian and Mexican support for this idea would have to be fought one at a time.

With Canada safely in the bag by the beginning of 1989, attention turned southward. Several years before, Mexico had undergone a wrenching debate over whether it should join the General Agreement on Tariffs and Trade, and many of the arguments resembled what Canadians would be hearing in their great trade debate. Those lining up in favour of Mexico's joining the GATT included young American-trained technocrats whose influence was growing in government ministries, while the opposition contained a bizarre alliance of left-wing intellectuals and the lazy owners of inefficient factories who have often passed for "industrialists" in Mexico.

The 1950s, 1960s and 1970s were a period of sustained economic growth for Mexico, transforming it from a mostly rural and agricultural country to an urbanized industrial society. One of the tools behind this change was a policy of import substitution whereby Mexican manufacturers enjoyed substantial tariff and quota protection along with tight restrictions on foreign ownership. Without much foreign competition, there was little to stop them from offering shoddy and overpriced goods to a captive domestic market. But in the early 1980s things began to go badly wrong. Recession in the western world, collapsing oil prices and crippling debt pummelled the Mexican economy, sending inflation and unemployment soaring while wages fell in real terms by more than one third. Something had to give. President López Portillo nationalized the entire banking industry just before leaving office in 1982 in an attempt to mask his appalling economic legacy, but his two successors, Miguel de la Madrid and Carlos Salinas de Gortari, took a very different tack.

After several years of improvisation and indecision, de la Madrid began to set Mexico on a more laissez-faire economic course, steering it into the GATT and loosening controls on imports and foreign ownership. Salinas, whose Harvard degree in economics was meant to impress, continued in the same vein and denationalized many state-owned companies, including some of the banks. Imported goods soon abounded in Mexican department stores and supermarkets, and Mexican debt purchased on the secondary market enabled foreigners to buy cheaply into the local economy.

With modest rises in investment and sharp rises in non-oil exports, it looked as though the tide might be turning and the economy might be poised for a new period of growth. But it was all happening too slowly to meet the demands of a burgeoning labour force. Something more dramatic was needed. When Brian Mulroney came visiting in March 1990, he bragged about the marvels of his trade deal with the U.S., and in so doing he drew Salinas into the open on his own desire to see something similar for Mexico. But when Mexico and the U.S. began formal talks, Canadian officials hesitated before finally deciding that they indeed wanted Mexico as a free trade partner.

At this point the whole chronology gets somewhat sticky. In fact, though the issue went public during Mulroney's visit to Mexico, Salinas had been telling anyone who would listen that he wanted a deal with the U.S. patterned after the Canada-U.S. deal. It also appears that preliminary discussions were well advanced since various Bush Administration officials, including the secretary of commerce, were testifying before both the Senate and the House of Representatives that a U.S.-Mexico deal was in the bag.

Moreover, Canada's relationship with the talks were problematic. We knew they were going on. Derek Burney, the Mr. Fixit of the U.S.-Canada deal, was now our ambassador to Washington, and he was keeping a worried watching brief on the various talks, but neither the U.S. nor Mexico seemed interested in inviting Canada to participate. The United States in particular wanted Canada out at least for the moment because some of the elements of the FTA could not be applied in the new talks. For example, if the agreement is to grow incrementally to cover the whole of the Americas as the expansive President Salinas seems to indicate, then the U.S. had little interest in easing the freedom of movement and immigration procedures that are part of the Canadian arrangement. On the other hand, the issue of the protection of "cultural industries" is not as pressing in Spanish-speaking America. A deal worked out between the U.S. and Mexico will likely reflect this difference, and it could then be put on the table for the upcoming negotiations between Canada and the U.S. Thus, when Mexico and the U.S. began formal talks, Canadian officials did not seem to know quite how to react.

All through Canada's free trade debate, Mulroney assured his audiences that the deal would give Canadian exporters preferred access to the U.S. market. If other countries also have preferred access, that erases part of the advantage Canadians were promised. The U.S. trade deal with Canada and a future deal with Mexico could remain bilateral, or they could be brought together to form a trilateral deal, in which case Canada would allow freer access to Mexican goods in exchange for enhanced access to the more populous but poorer Mexican market. After Mulroney helped sell the Mexican public on the merits of free trade, his government initially seemed befuddled by the forces he had played a minor role in unleashing.

The Mulroney government was worried — and others were worried a whole lot more — by the prospect of job loss in Canada. A day's industrial wages in Mexico are about equal to an hour's wages in Canada, which may help explain why Canadians working for a list of companies that included General Motors, Ford, Chrysler, General Electric, Westinghouse, Black and Decker, Johnson and Johnson, Eastman Kodak and Campbell Soup suffered layoffs while these same companies opened new export-oriented plants in northern Mexico.

The problem for post-free trade Canada is that worrying is about the only thing the government can do. Of course, the Canadian government never had any power to determine the corporate policies of foreign-controlled companies and could never have expressed any opinion about where they decided to build their factories. Nor has it ever presumed to have any say over what American trade policy would be. But before free trade we could influence, at least to a degree, our own international trade policy and our own market. We cannot do this any more. If the U.S. and Mexico enter an arrangement that would allow GM, for example, to move goods duty-free across the Mexico-U.S. border, we cannot stop GM from moving those same goods freely across the U.S.-Canada border. Because of our integrated economy, anybody who has a free trade arrangement with the U.S. has one, for all practical purposes, with Canada.

If multinationals operating in Canada can take full advantage of any Mexico-U.S. free trade, it is natural that any remaining indigenous manufacturers should do likewise. To whatever degree a region in North America may have cheap labour and other advantages to attract investment, investment will flow to the region in that same degree. That's how competition works. One clothing manufacturer in Montreal, asked in 1988 how free trade might affect his Canadian operations, said he was not especially worried about competition from the U.S., but he was pleased that no similar deal was being signed then with a low-wage country.

The evolving global division of labour suggests that high-wage countries such as Canada should be moving upmarket into higher-end goods and more advanced production techniques while leaving simpler, more labour-intensive tasks to the Third World. That looks interesting in theory but shows a naïve confidence in Canada's technical and entrepreneurial skills and an unwarranted faith in its severely deficient job retraining programs.

Meanwhile, a special form of free trade has operated for decades along Mexico's border with the United States. Under a scheme initiated in the 1960s but vastly expanded in recent years, U.S. companies can send components to Mexican plants for assembly without paying Mexican duty and can then re-import the finished goods virtually free of U.S. duty. These in-bond assembly operations, commonly known as maquiladoras, are heavily concentrated in Tijuana, Ciudad Juárez and several smaller cities along the border. Although work is more abundant and wages often higher than in other parts of Mexico, families often live in utter squalor because of severe housing shortages. In theory *maquiladora* plants can be situated almost anywhere in Mexico, but placing them at the border allows manufacturers to benefit from low wages without having to deal extensively with Mexican highways or the vagaries of Mexican telephones.

At first most *maquiladoras* were American-owned, but more recently Japanese firms have poured in, partly in response to anti-Asian protectionist moves in the U.S. Congress and partly in response to rising wage costs in Asia. Relatively few *maquiladoras* have gone to Tamaulipas state in northeastern Mexico because of its strong union tradition, but some firms have begun to discover that a unionized work force is often a more stable work force; many nonunionized plants further west have been plagued by high worker turnover.

The *maquiladora* system can continue to function under current rules, but it depends for its long-term survival on some sort of comprehensive trade deal with the U.S. (Canada would merely be an adornment). Inevitably the *maquiladoras* will look to Mexican suppliers for a growing proportion of their components, and when that happens they risk losing their duty-free status in the U.S. — unless a trade deal is in place. Mexico needs more jobs, and the U.S. wants more Mexicans employed at home to relieve pressure on its porous southern border.

For Canada these concerns are more remote. But the *maquiladora* phenomenon by no means tells the whole story of new industrial development in Mexico. A wave of automakers and other heavy manufacturers has found Mexico fertile ground for the production of engines and other parts as well as vehicles for export. But with much of the available skilled labour and management talent already skimmed off by existing employers, it is an open question whether future waves of investment will have as easy a time. What remains in greatest abundance is unskilled labour.

It may seem churlish of highly paid Canadians to begrudge a few extra jobs to needy Mexicans, and in any case their worst fears will not necessarily come true. Trade agreements can help spur exports, but they are not a *sine qua non*: South Korea and Taiwan became powerful trading countries without enjoying privileged access to wealthier markets. Despite recent improvements, Mexico has not been a leader in global trade, and a few signatures on a fancy piece of paper are not going to transform it into something it hasn't been. Yes, some investment will continue to shift southward, and yes, it will cost some jobs in Canada, but many of the jobs being created in Mexico might otherwise have gone to low-wage Asian countries such as Thailand, Malaysia, Indonesia or China whose workers are even less likely than Mexicans to buy Canadian goods. Any job loss in Canada hurts, but in an era when factories can be moved around the world like chess pieces, a treaty linking Canada and Mexico will not make a vast difference. The prospect of becoming part of Region North America is not so much the huge economic threat that some Canadians fear as an indication of the kind of world in which Canada is being asked to make sense of itself.

Meech Lake (1): The Agreement That Wasn't

The aftermath of the Canada-U.S. Free Trade Agreement, including the possibility or threat of a deal between the United States and Mexico, became overshadowed in 1989 and 1990 by questions of Canada's internal constitution — both in the narrow sense of the piece of paper under which Canada is governed and in the broader sense of the way the country is constituted. It was not entirely a coincidence that a constitutional crisis erupted in Canada within months of the signing of the FTA. Indeed, the controversy over the Meech Lake Accord acquired levels of meaning that were largely caused by the new political conditions created in Canada by the FTA, although it took some time for the relationship between the two developments to become clear.

To a large extent, the deeper political issues that came to be subsumed under the heading "Meech Lake" surfaced only in the later stages of the debate on ratification of the accord, and especially after the signing of the FTA in 1989. But the misunderstandings that eventually brought down the accord itself were built into it from the beginning in 1987. There were at least four such misunderstandings: regarding native people, the nature of Manitoba's commitment to the accord, the relationship between Quebec's position and that of the other provinces, and the process by which it is appropriate for Canada to amend its constitution.

The First Nations were among the most seriously aggrieved people when the Meech deal was announced, not least because of the contrast between what happened at Meech Lake and what had occurred at another constitutional conference barely a month earlier. This was the last in a series of conferences arising out of the 1982 constitution that were to engage the question of aboriginal self-government, and it ended, as had all the others, in failure. As Ottawa commentator Adam Zachary wrote in July 1987, "From the federal point of view, spending the political capital required for a native agreement would have left little in the bank for the constitutional negotiations that really mattered electorally — the talks that took place in April on Quebec's status within Confederation." As it turned out, however, putting a little political capital into reaching an accommodation with the First Nations would not have been quite so frivolous an investment for Ottawa as it seemed at the time.

A second misunderstanding concerns the extent to which there was an agreement at Meech Lake and the Langevin Block in 1987 at all, at least in the sense in which it was presented to the country in subsequent weeks and months. One of the premiers who was most hesitant to sign the detailed agreement that emerged from the Langevin Block meeting was Howard Pawley of Manitoba. Pawley was nervous about the accord's dilution of federal powers, especially the spending power, and its possible effect on future social programs. As writer Andrew Cohen later reconstructed the scene:

"Pawley said he was unhappy, but that he would hold public hearings as required by provincial law. He warned that his agreement was conditional, but agree he did .... 'I'm signing this,' he said. 'But you should know my reservations. If those public hearings give me additional concerns, I'll be back at the table. They will not be a rubber stamp."

In other words, Pawley's approval had much the same character as that of his successor, Gary Filmon, three years later. It was reluctant and subject to approval through a reasonably democratic process in Manitoba. Opposition to the accord developed quickly. Reports that Pawley's NDP government was preparing to withdraw its support of the accord were already floating around Winnipeg in early 1988, before they were made irrelevant by the defeat of the government in the legislature and the subsequent provincial election. That election (which prompted the new opposition leader, Sharon Carstairs, to pronounce the accord "dead"), the 1988 federal election (which emboldened opponents of the accord within the NDP by failing to produce an NDP breakthrough in Quebec), Quebec's sign law and Premier Filmon's reaction to it in early 1989, the provincial task force's public hearings and subsequent report, and — finally — MLA Elijah Harper's insistence that the province's rules for amending the constitution be followed were all steps in the demise of Meech Lake in Manitoba. But the seeds of its destruction were there from the beginning.

Andrew Cohen also identifies another major misunderstanding that would later have serious consequences. It was Quebec's exclusion from the 1981 constitutional deal that made the Meech round of negotiations necessary, and it was the accession of more accommodating governments in Ottawa in 1984 and Quebec City in 1985 that made it possible. Brian Mulroney promised to have Quebec sign the constitution "with honour and enthusiasm," and the government of Robert Bourassa formulated five conditions for doing precisely that: a say in choosing Supreme Court justices, more powers over immigration, a veto over constitutional amendments, limitation of the federal spending power and recognition as a distinct society. The Edmonton Declaration of August 1986 signalled a willingness on the part of all the premiers to make the next round of constitutional discussions a Quebec round. Quebec's five conditions would be the basis for negotiation, and no further amendments would be considered until these conditions were dealt with.

As a way of proceeding, this had considerable merit. Ottawa and the other nine provinces had, after all, already signed the constitution. Even the constitutional demands of such groups as women and native people had had at least an echo in the 1981-82 deal. The problem before the first ministers was the exclusion of Quebec, and Bourassa's five conditions represented a way of solving that problem neatly and surgically.

But by the time the constitutional caravan made camp on the shores of Meech Lake in April 1987, the commitment to deal only with Quebec's conditions had been left in the ditch. "On the way to Meech Lake," writes Cohen, "the Quebec Round (as it was originally called) had become the provincial round. The premiers would make much of the spirit of compromise at Meech Lake, but Alberta had already served notice that it would reject the deal if it could not advance Senate reform. Newfoundland wanted something on fisheries, while British Columbia eyed property rights. The commitment to focus exclusively on Quebec had faded like a soft summer mist." The other provinces also wanted the new powers that Quebec would get out of the deal to apply to themselves as well. The ambiguity in the deal as it emerged from the Langevin Block was perhaps best indicated by two phrases: the proposed amendment that sought to entrench "the recognition that Quebec constitutes within Canada a distinct society" and the phrase in the political statement accompanying the amendments that "would recognize the principle of equality of all the provinces."

For Quebec, it did not much matter how the rest of the country arranged its affairs, so long as its five conditions were met. Whether Saskatchewan could nominate Supreme Court justices, British Columbia had a veto over constitutional change or Prince Edward Island had more powers over immigration were outside Quebec's concern. In the eyes of Premier Bourassa and of most Quebecers who followed such matters, the Meech round not only began as a Quebec round; it remained one. This was part of the basis for the equation that was made with increasing frequency as the three-year effort to ratify Meech ran its course: rejection of Meech Lake meant rejection of Quebec.

In the rest of Canada, however, there was far from universal agreement among people who didn't happen to be provincial premiers on the additional provisions that were thrown into the Meech Lake deal. Some of the opposition to the accord focused on the distinct society clause (especially its relation to the Charter of Rights) and other provisions arising specifically out of Quebec's demands. But there was also opposition based on features of the accord that were not at all inherent in the five conditions. Thus, some people objected to the accord's overall decentralizing thrust, particularly in light of the free trade agreement and the need that many people saw for more federal power to protect Canadian sovereignty. Others argued that requiring unanimity for some forms of constitutional change that had previously required the approval only of the federal government and seven provinces representing at least 50 per cent of the population would make the constitutional reform process unnecessarily rigid. This was especially so in the case of the admission of new provinces: many people in the Yukon and Northwest Territories saw the unanimity requirement as representing a permanent block to provincial status.

Thus, the shift from a Quebec to a provincial agenda, far from creating a consensus on the accord outside Quebec, gave people additional reasons to oppose it. And their opposition would be seen as, and would effectively be, a rejection of Quebec, even where that was not their intent.

The debate about Meech Lake focused as much on process as it did on substance. The image of eleven white middle-aged men sitting in a closed room deciding our constitutional future was at least as powerful a weapon in Meech opponents' arsenal as was the distinct society clause or unanimity. This focus on process was appropriate, since constitutions are largely about process: they are supposed to set guidelines for the conduct of a country's public affairs.

Until 1982, there was no indigenous process for amending the Canadian constitution; as an act of the British Parliament, the British North America Act could be amended only by that Parliament. In theory, the British MPs and lords could amend the BNA Act whenever they felt like it, but in practice they would do so only in response to a request from Canada. What constituted a valid request from Canada was not entirely clear, and much of the legal wrangling between the Trudeau government and the Gang of Eight turned on this question. While it could be argued that Canada functioned passably well without being able to amend its own constitution, the absence of a generally accepted amending procedure made it difficult to effect substantive change to the BNA Act, and it was widely believed that this could, at some point, be a serious problem.

It was this situation that the constitutional exercise of 1980-82 was designed to correct; while other changes such as the Charter of Rights were thrown into the package, adoption of an amending formula was what "patriation" was all about. The amending formula chosen was a rather complicated one, taking up twelve articles of the constitution and providing for a variety of amending procedures for different circumstances. Two of these procedures are relevant to Meech Lake. Most amendments to the constitution fall under subsection 38 (1):

> An amendment to the Constitution of Canada may be made by proclamation issued by the Governor General under the Great Seal of Canada where so authorized by
>
> > (a) resolutions of the Senate and the House of Commons; and
> >
> > (b) resolutions of the legislative assemblies of at least two-thirds of the provinces that have, in the aggregate, according to the then latest general census, at least fifty per cent of the population of all the provinces.

Subsection 39(2) specifies that:

> A proclamation shall not be issued under subsection 38(1) after the expiration of three years from the adoption of the resolution initiating the amendment procedure thereunder.

In some cases, however, consent of all the provinces is required rather than just of seven provinces with at least 50 per cent of the population. These are specified in section 41:

> An amendment to the Constitution of Canada in relation to the following matters may be made by proclamation issued by the Governor General under the Great Seal of Canada only where authorized by

resolutions of the Senate and House of Commons and of the legislative assembly of each province:

(a) the office of the Queen, the Governor General and the Lieutenant Governor of a province;

(b) the right of a province to a number of members in the House of Commons not less than the number of Senators by which the province is entitled to be represented at the time this Part comes into force;

(c) ... the use of the English or the French language;

(d) the composition of the Supreme Court of Canada; and

(e) an amendment to this Part.

No time limit is specified for amendments under section 41. Thus, for some amendments, the approval of seven provinces and the federal government is required within three years. For others, unanimous consent is required, but with no time limit. Nowhere is there any provision for a unanimity requirement combined with a three-year time limit. And yet this was precisely the procedure followed with the Meech Lake Accord.

The reasons for adhering to the three-year limit remain a bit of a mystery, although they clearly relate to the decision to treat the amendments that made up the Meech Lake Accord as a "package" that had to be passed in its entirety or not at all. The accord itself is vague about the procedure to be followed in ratifying it, the only reference being a "whereas" in the "Motion for a Resolution to authorize an amendment to the Constitution of Canada" that precedes the actual amendments: "AND WHEREAS certain portions of the amendment proposed in the schedule hereto relate to matters referred to in section 41 of the *Constitution Act, 1982*." The next *whereas* goes on to spell out exactly what section 41 says. But as we have seen, nowhere is there a provision for a time limit for amendments under section 41.

Since some of the Meech Lake amendments do not relate to matters referred to in section 41, the first ministers may have felt that the three-year time limit applied to these amendments and therefore to the whole package. But Gordon Robertson, clerk of the Privy Council and constitutional adviser under Pierre Trudeau, believed otherwise: that since Meech Lake was being handled according to section 41, in strictly legal terms there was no time limit. In political terms, however, the time limit had become a very real one, at least by late 1989.

Also absent from the constitution is any requirement that a first ministers' meeting be held to discuss a constitutional amendment. Because the process — especially the closed first ministers' meeting and the take-it-or-leave-it deal that meeting produced — came under such severe criticism, some Meech supporters were forced into a defence of the process. The most ardent defender was Premier Bourassa. Meech Lake had to be passed, Bourassa said on numerous occasions, to protect the sanctity of the process. What was a premier's signature worth if the people of his province could overturn an agreement he had signed? Others, such as Prime Minister Mulroney and former NDP leader Ed Broadbent, conceded that the process might have flaws but argued that it had been inherited and that this was not the time to change the rules of the game. In fact, however, the 1980-82 process, while no model of democracy, had contained elements of openness not present in 1987-90. And furthermore, the whole purpose of the 1980-82 exercise had been to change the rules of the game by establishing an amending procedure that could be applied in Canada with general consent.

Meech Lake signalled the failure of that exercise. As it turned out, there was no effective amending procedure, any more than there had been before 1982. Instead of following the script laid down in the 1982 constitution, the first ministers improvised, all the more frantically as the hoots of derision from the audience became louder. It was as if they were trying to play a baseball game without first having agreed on where the foul lines were, whether there would be seven innings or nine, and whether the pitcher could be replaced at bat by a designated hitter.

And yet, if it had only been a question of agreeing on the rules in this narrow sense, the Meech Lake affair would never have taken on the proportions that it did. Failed attempts at constitutional amendment are not in themselves critical for a country. It is revealing that after toying with describing what was involved in Meech Lake as a "constitutional crisis," commentators ultimately settled on the broader term "psychodrama." While this term was perhaps not quite accurate either, placing too much emphasis on psychological factors rather than political and economic ones, it at least had the merit of recognizing that the constitutional arguments were no more than the surface of what was happening.

In his forever frustrated efforts to catch the Road Runner, in the Warner Brothers' cartoons, Wile E. Coyote sometimes runs over a cliff. No matter; he just keeps running — until he looks down. When he sees only the abyss below him, he stops and falls to the bottom. Through most of the Meech Lake operation, Canadians thought they were still on the road. But slowly, through late 1989 and early 1990, they began to look down.

7

Beyond the Nation-State

As we have seen, there was both a current and a historical dimension to the crisis that was gathering force under the surface in Canada in 1989. A weak federal state, a diminished freedom of action relative to the United States, a decreasing sense of common interest among Canadians — all were the logical outcome of a myriad of decisions, explicit and implicit, taken since 1945. But they were also helped along by the presence in Ottawa of a government that was enamoured of the bottom line and consciously rejected any consideration of a Canadian "national interest."

There was yet another dimension to Canada's situation, an international one, whose scope would become clear before 1989 ran its course. Canada was far from being the only country where groups distinct by virtue of language, territory and historical consciousness were seeking new arrangements. Nor was North America the only continent where countries were moving towards closer economic ties. Events in eastern and western Europe, in particular, suggested that what was happening in Canada was shaped by global as well as local developments. For a good part of 1989, however, not much appeared to be happening in Canada at all.

Why Was Brian Mulroney Smiling?

Brian Mulroney's mood as he returned to Ottawa from the NATO anniversary summit meeting in Brussels in June 1989 was upbeat. Even on the surface, the situation he was returning to was not a happy one. Parliament was outraged by a budget leak that had grown into a tangle of criminal charges. Political stonewalling had led to charges of conscious coverup, and bureaucratic incompetence had grown into government interference with justice.

Meanwhile, one former Tory member of Parliament had just got out of jail and was working at a halfway house in the Ottawa area, another had been sentenced on a conviction of fraud and breach of trust and a third was about to go on trial. Mulroney's Quebec campaign chair, Senator Michel Cogger, already mixed up in a multimillion-dollar lawsuit involving charges of influence peddling, was named by a senior federal bureaucrat as ordering him to "get moving" on a $45-million funding request for one of his clients.

Opponents of the free trade deal pounced on every layoff, plant closing and takeover — and there were many — as evidence of the deal's noxious effects. The government denied that any of these developments had the remotest connection with free trade. The lengthening lines of cars at major border points taking Canadians to the United States to do their shopping stood as a symbol of the new order. This, too, had nothing to do with free trade.

The government was getting sad news from the polls: down to about 36 per cent and falling, with the biggest decline in its power base in Quebec. Worse was still to come as the impact of the Wilson budget was beginning to be measured — one prominent brokerage firm had already predicted a massive drop in the value of southern Ontario real estate, which would trigger an abrupt decline in economic activity, spreading across the country and developing into a full-blown recession by early 1990 — all because of the budget. The Economic Council of Canada was about to announce that the new Goods and Services Tax would lead to higher unemployment and that the proposed 9 per cent rate for 1991 would soon rise. Both the CBC and Via Rail were at work choosing the hemlock they had been ordered to drink.

Why then was the prime minister relaxed and jovial with the press at the back of the plane heading from Brussels?

One reporter accompanying the prime minister attributed his upbeat mood to the lesson he had learned during his first term: that a majority victory assures carte blanche. This is usually true even when the parliamentary opposition isn't impotent and discredited, as it was in the summer of 1989. The intensity of the free trade debate had faded; the Meech Lake ratification deadline was still a year away. A Supreme Court decision mandating bilingual commercial signs had led to a renewed language controversy in Quebec that refused to die down, but Quebec language controversies were a normal part of the Canadian political scene. Canadians appeared to be most concerned with the environment, and Mulroney had assigned this important portfolio to the rising star of his cabinet, Lucien Bouchard.

As the summer wore on, the prime minister seemed even more detached from affairs of state. A few speeches on Meech Lake, an announcement that the next federal-provincial conference on the accord would be postponed to get Quebec Premier Robert Bourassa past his fall election and to give the federal Liberals more time to strangle on the accord as they began their leadership contest, on his merry way for photo opportunities with Margaret Thatcher, over to François Mitterrand's Bicentenary gala, and then home to rest up for his fall trip to Asia. It was summer, after all, and nobody appeared much concerned with affairs of government, least of all our prime minister.

Meech Lake (2): The Hole under the Political Surface

The minor scandals, the disappointing poll results, the budget leak controversy, the rumours of recession, the plant closings, even the difficulty of selling the primacy of deficit reduction to a skeptical public — all these were, at most, symptoms of Mulroney's deeper problem. In the strange political calm of the first two thirds of 1989, the fundamental rationale for the existence of the government Mulroney headed was fatally weakened.

Canada was not the only country undergoing such a development. In the early fall, Mikhail Gorbachev travelled to East Berlin to join the longtime head of East Germany's Communist Party, Erich Honecker, in celebration of the fortieth anniversary of Communist government in that country. Already, however, thousands of East Germans were streaming towards the West, making an end run around the Berlin Wall via the border between Hungary and Austria which had become easier to cross as political change in Hungary took hold.

Within days Honecker would be deposed as leader, by November the wall would start coming down, a new non-Communist government would be elected early in 1990, and less than a year later East Germany would have gone out of business as a distinct country.

The gaping hole beneath the political surface was not quite as conspicuous in Canada as in East Germany, nor would the reasons for its existence be as easily identifiable. Nevertheless, by the spring of 1990 the weakness of their country's sovereignty and what was euphemistically termed its national unity would be clear to a growing number of Canadians, and this realization would colour the gathering debate over the Meech Lake Accord.

As the perception of Canadian vulnerability gained strength, a number of versions of the events that had brought the new situation about were formulated. The most widely accepted version in English Canada placed most of the blame on Quebec Premier Robert Bourassa and traced the origin of the crisis to Bill 178, Bourassa's restrictive language legislation passed early in 1989. In this version, Bill 178 sparked opposition to Meech Lake in English Canada, led Gary Filmon to abandon his support of the accord, and ultimately provoked the "English-only" resolutions adopted in Sault Sainte-Marie, Thunder Bay and dozens of other Ontario towns that soured the political atmosphere and made ratification of Meech Lake impossible.

Undoubtedly, large numbers of English Canadians took a dim view of Bill 178, and the chances of creating the atmosphere of goodwill in which Meech Lake might have served not only as a means of securing Quebec's signature on the constitution but also as an instrument of genuine reconciliation between French and English Canadians were thereby diminished. Focusing on Bill 178 also has the merit of singling out an event that occurred at the time — early 1989 — when the current phase of Canada's disintegration did in fact begin. Nevertheless, Bill 178 does not come near to providing an adequate explanation for the events that followed, let alone the deeper crisis that those events revealed.

First of all, Canada had lived for more than eleven years with restrictions on English signs in Quebec that were, on the whole, more severe than those mandated in Bill 178. The PQ's 1977 Charter of the French Language (Bill 101) had prohibited both indoor and outdoor commercial signs in languages other than French. When the Supreme Court of Canada declared this provision unconstitutional in December 1988, Bourassa's Bill 178, which overrode the Supreme Court decision on the basis of the "notwithstanding" clause in the 1982 constitution, prohibited only outdoor signs (although it also removed an exemption for companies with fewer than five employees that had been contained in Bill 101).

Second, Meech Lake was already unpopular in Manitoba; Filmon, in charge of a precarious minority government, was looking for an excuse to detach himself from the accord and prevent defeat at the hands of Meech Lake's most implacable opponent, Sharon Carstairs, then at the zenith of her meteoric political career. And Filmon's logic in associating his reversal on Meech Lake with Bill 178 was more than a little tortured. It wasn't Bill 178 itself that had forced his decision, Filmon argued, but the fact that Bourassa had said that if Meech Lake had been in effect he would have used its distinct society clause rather than the notwithstanding clause to override the Supreme Court decision; this had alerted Filmon, he said, to the dangers of the distinct society clause. But if Quebec — or any other province (it was, after all, Manitoba that had initially insisted on the notwithstanding clause) — already had the means to override the Charter of Rights, what made Meech Lake so dangerous?

No single factor fully accounts for the change in Canadian politics that took hold in 1989 and that would manifest itself in the Meech Lake debate — and, in different ways, in the standoff at Oka, the September 1990 Ontario election and the battle over the Goods and Services Tax. In some respects, it was not a change at all, but rather the culmination of developments that had been taking place since the Second World War: having pursued postwar prosperity through continental integration, having sought special treatment from the United States at almost every turn, having failed to deal with regional grievances, having failed to develop a vision of the country that accommodated not only the French language but some form of Quebec nationalism, having failed even more deeply to develop a vision of the country that had room for the aspirations of native people, Canada was now paying the price.

But Canada did cross a threshold early in 1989, and probably the best place to look for clues to the nature of this threshold is the federal election of 1988, the circumstances under which it was fought and won by the Conservatives, and the free trade deal that emanated from it.

Although in the beginning only John Turner and the Pro-Canada Network wanted to fight the election on free trade, in the end that was the issue everyone had to fight on: not only the Liberals, Conservatives and NDP but also the big guns of Canadian business, who wanted the deal very badly. While support for the deal ebbed and flowed (mostly ebbed), a consistent sentiment among Canadians was that they didn't have enough information about it. The Conservatives' strategy of seeking not to explain the deal but to "sell" it contributed to this sentiment. Meanwhile, both sides played to deep fears in the electorate: the anti-free trade side to fears of losing Canadian sovereignty and social programs, the pro-free traders to fears of being left out in a world where vast trade blocs were forming and the United States was retreating into a protectionist shell. Many Canadians came to see the country's future as being at stake in the election, and the side that presented itself as the champion of Canadian sovereignty lost. But while business intervention in the late stages of the campaign may have succeeded in settling the matter according to the rules of the electoral game, it did not succeed in putting people's fears to rest. Rather, these fears stayed alive into 1989, seeking new outlets and affecting different issues.

A major complicating factor was the extent to which the election was decided in Quebec. A few figures are salient here. The percentage of the popular vote the Tories won outside Quebec in 1988 was lower than in any election since the Trudeaumania sweep of 1968. The percentage of seats the Tories won outside Quebec was also lower than at any time since 1968, although it was only marginally lower than in the 1974 and 1980 elections — both of which resulted in Liberal majorities. By any measure, Tory support outside Quebec was far lower than in the Tory good years of 1972, 1979 and 1984. In comparison with 1984, Tory support outside Quebec was down by 10 per cent, while in Quebec it was up by almost 2 per cent. And finally, had the Tories been able to win as many seats in Quebec in other elections as they did in 1988, they would have won every election since 1957, all except 1968 with majorities.

In other words, virtually the whole difference between the 1988 election and the elections of the Pearson and Trudeau eras that gave us Liberal governments was the switch from Liberal to Conservative dominance of Quebec. In Quebec, support for the Tories in 1988 was broad and enthusiastic; outside Quebec it was spotty and grudging. If the 1988 election was about the future of the country, that future appeared very different from the perspective of Halifax, Hamilton or Regina than it did from Chicoutimi, Quebec City or Laval.

The 1988 election did not represent the first time that voters in Quebec pursued a different agenda from those in English Canada. Thus in 1972, when a loss of forty-six seats in English Canada brought Pierre Trudeau to the brink of defeat, the number of Liberal seats in Quebec remained unchanged. And in 1979, the year Trudeau lost to Joe Clark, a decline of thirty-four Liberal seats in English Canada was partly offset by a *gain* of seven seats in Quebec, mostly from the fading Créditistes. One common interpretation of these results at the time (and especially in 1979) was that Quebec had cast a "family" vote, lining up behind one of its own. A similar spin could be placed on the 1988 results, with the only difference being that this time Quebec's favourite son was the Tory Brian Mulroney instead of the Liberal Pierre Trudeau.

However, free trade was also a significant component of the difference in perspective. There was opposition to free trade in Quebec, but it was concentrated on the economic effects of the deal; as in the rest of the country there would be both winners and losers under free trade. What was different was the interplay between opposition to free trade and national-ism. In English Canada, economic opposition was supported by Canadian nationalist opposition, for which the Liberal cam-paign made a strong pitch — perhaps most memorably in Turner's exchange with Mulroney in the English-language leaders' debate and in the television commercial showing free trade negotiators erasing the Canada-U.S. border.

In Quebec, by contrast, economic opposition was undercut by Quebec nationalist support for the deal, based on both the historic pro-American stance of mainstream Quebec nationalism and the rise of Quebec business in the 1980s. Both the Quebec Liberal Party and the Parti Québécois supported the deal (each for its own reasons), as did Quebec intellectuals of nearly all persuasions. While there was a surge in support for the Liberals in Quebec in the wake of the leaders' debates just as there was in English Canada, it neither went as far nor lasted as long. By the end of the campaign, the Tories had more than captured back the support they had lost in Quebec.

In 1972 and 1979, people who saw the electoral split between Quebec and the rest of the country as dangerous had responded by explaining the split away, pretending it didn't exist, or ignoring it. But the 1988 split was of a different order, and the response in English Canada was different as well. Among English Canadian opponents of free trade, some of whom had previously been sympathetic to Quebec nationalism, there was a sense of having been betrayed by Quebec, expressed most vehemently by University of British Columbia political scientist Philip Resnick in his *Letters to a Québécois Friend*:

> You voted in this election with supreme indifference to the issues of both Canadian identity and appropriate models of society so clearly posed in the rest of Canada. What mattered to your political elites (and their big business backers) were the gains (real or hypothetical) that Quebec stood to make from the deal. You were ostensibly insulated by language and culture from American influence (I think you greatly underestimate the dangers you face), and would in any case take action to protect *your* national identity were it threatened, witness your government's action following the Supreme Court judgment. But towards *our* national identity (or the question of moderately egalitarian versus neo-conservative choices) your attitude bespoke a sacred egoism bordering on contempt.

It is not difficult to find weaknesses in Resnick's argument. He exaggerates both the sympathy in English Canada for Quebec nationalism and the obligation for Quebecers to set aside their own agenda to support English Canada's "national project." We have seen how the Quebec nationalist André Laurendeau became sensitive to the importance of pursuing the task of redefining Quebec's place in Confederation in the context of American domination of Canada and the stirrings of resistance in English Canada to that domination. But, as we have also seen, that path was not seriously followed in either Quebec or English Canada. In particular, English Canadian nationalists of the left, while making the right sympathetic noises towards Quebec's national aspirations, never devoted much thought to the question of how those aspirations fit in with their own vision of an independent Canada. In that context, it is hardly surprising that Quebec nationalists should be somewhat skeptical of English Canadian sympathy (which was confined to a small minority in any case) or that they should look at the free trade deal in terms of Quebec interests. Quebec and English Canadian nationalists might have built bridges in the 1960s; after two decades of pursuing separate paths, it was far too late in 1988.

But even if the feeling of betrayal to which Resnick gave voice rested on shaky foundations, it was nonetheless real. And it was one more element in the volatile atmosphere in which the Meech Lake ratification debate would take place, along with the doubts about Canada's long-term viability fostered by free trade, Quebec's determination to pursue its own destiny without much regard for the rest of Canada, the prime minister's taste for pursuing his ends through manipulation and back-room deals, the government's growing indebtedness and consequent lack of room to manoeuvre, and the approach of a recession whose impending arrival was announced daily in the media.

To be sure, a Turner government committed to tearing up the free trade deal would have faced many of the same problems, some in the same form and others in mirror image: a business elite that would quickly move towards other ways of getting what it wanted, a Quebec that would see its agenda being derailed by English Canada once again. Canada after the free trade debate would have been a very different country from what it was before even if free trade had been defeated. As it turned out, however, the final stages of the Meech Lake ratification process were to be carried out with the free trade deal in place and with Brian Mulroney and his Conservatives still on the government benches in Ottawa.

The Weakening of Sovereign States

Just suppose, for a moment, that Quebec did finally go ahead and secede from Canada. Imagine that the unthinkable had become the inevitable and two sovereign states now existed where most maps still showed only Canada. It would not be the first time in history a country had broken apart, nor would it be the last. But it would be happening at a time when the world was starting to reshape its concepts of nation and state.

Some of the old concepts of national sovereignty are starting to come under pressure from two concurrent and seemingly opposite tendencies: an upsurge in secessionism and the growth of trading blocs. Nowhere is this truer than in Canada, and the world will be watching to see how Canada adjusts. Will Canada build a model to be imitated, or might it be a catastrophe to be avoided?

In more than a few respects, Canada has been one of the most successful countries the twentieth century has witnessed. In economic terms, it has provided most of its people with standards of living and levels of opportunity that few other countries have matched. In social and cultural terms, it has built state-financed networks of education, health and income support services that, despite their flaws, are the envy of most foreigners. Canada's vastness and natural abundance have confounded even the wanton carelessness of its environmental practices. Its cities, among the safest and cleanest in the western hemisphere, have absorbed different racial and cultural groups more harmoniously than cities in many other places. And in political terms, Canada has often seemed to outsiders to be a country so peaceful and tolerant that it has had to invent its internal disputes. Political challenges have tended to be met with a minimum of rancour or violence.

Yet Canada may have steered itself onto a path that imperils its ability to survive the century intact. If a country this

successful — and a glance around the globe reveals a distress-
ingly long list of countries that have mismanaged their affairs
even more egregiously than Canada has — cannot hold things
together, what prospects lie in store for the internal unity of
the many countries with shakier economies, more heterogeneous populations and shabbier treatment of minorities?

At a time when economic boundaries between countries are
being torn asunder for the greater glory of world trade, will
the 1990s also see a realignment of political boundaries in
response to the tugs and thrusts of conflicting nationalisms?
Could Canada unwittingly end up being a pioneer in an impending worldwide redefinition of the relation between nation
and state?

Stepping back a generation or so, to the time when Robert
Stanfield was the new leader of the federal Conservatives, we
saw a political party casting about awkwardly trying to re-
build its pathetically shrunken base of support in Quebec.
Stanfield had called on the intellectual services of a Montreal
financier named Marcel Faribault, who proposed the far from
novel concept that Canada was a country made up of two
nations, one English-speaking and the other French-speaking.

Unfortunately for Stanfield and his hapless Quebec
lieutenant, this was a time when the Quebec independence
movement was just beginning to make serious inroads in the
consciousness of English Canada. And Canadians were
scarcely interested in academic discussions of the distinction
between nation and country, which in North American English usage had come to be almost synonymous. Americans had
no hesitation in referring to their country as "the nation";
indeed, despite their regional, racial and cultural differences,
Americans saw themselves very much as forming a single
nation, an idea drilled into their minds at least since the end
of the Civil War.

Even the United States, with its strong ideological under-
pinning of nationhood, has not been immune to the pressures
of regional particularism and ethnic assertiveness. But its concept of nationhood had spilled across the border into a different country where it applied much less readily, and when
Faribault defended his two-nations theory during the 1968
election campaign, the archcentralist Pierre Trudeau had little

trouble making him sound like a protoseparatist who wanted to split the Canadian "nation" in two. Trudeau's ascendancy laid the two-nations approach to constitution-building to rest for a generation.

In many places outside North America, nation and country (or state) are easily understood as separate concepts. The English, Welsh, Northern Irish and Scots have no trouble recognizing each other as distinct nations with their own territories, traditions and characteristics. They even send separate national teams to world sporting events. But they all belong to the same sovereign state, the United Kingdom of Great Britain and Northern Ireland. Yet many Canadians who trace their origins to England or Scotland have trouble accepting the idea that Quebec should be recognized as a distinct society, even a "nation," within the Canadian state.

It may be of little comfort to proponents of Canadian unity to know that other countries also face secessionist threats that could one day alter the world's political geography more radically than anything since the dismantling of the British and French colonial empires. Bloody civil conflicts have pitted Ethiopian central authorities against Eritreans and Tigreans, Iraqis against Kurds, Sinhalese against Tamils, Burmese against Karens, and so on down a long list of plurinational states where ethnic minorities have turned to force of arms in response to the discrimination and oppression they see emanating from distant capitals. Secessionist pressures have approached the bursting point in the Soviet Union and Yugoslavia as well, even if the casualty figures have not been nearly as appalling.

In an imperfect world, the imperfect concept of the nation-state has been applied in varied forms since ancient times. One of many problems with the nation-state idea is that there are far more nations than states. One United Nations study counted more than 2,500 national groups around the world but only 160 sovereign states. Of necessity, then, different national groups have had to coexist within the same boundaries, sometimes with happy results but often not. Where one group dominates, others may feel excluded from the exercise of sovereignty.

In a few special instances, the boundaries of nation and state do coincide. Sweden and Japan are readily recognizable as states whose boundaries encompass people of similar language, customs and origins, conforming to a classic dictionary definition of nation-state. But such examples are notable primarily for their rarity. France, while coming close to meeting this definition, has not managed fully to assimilate its Bretons and Corsicans. China's population is 93 per cent Han Chinese, but the remaining 7 per cent (representing a population roughly three times that of Canada) include Tibetans who have never accepted the brutal annexation of their homeland.

Far more common than the classic nation-state, and far less tidy, is the plurinational state, the foremost example being the Soviet Union with its fifteen republics and many autonomous regions, each one home to a separate nationality (but by no means accounting for all nationalities populating Soviet territory). Most African countries are patchwork quilts of different groups; Nigeria alone comprises about 250 ethnic groups, each occupying an identifiable territory. Since the drawing of borders has often been an arbitrary process (and not just in Africa), they often seem off kilter; thus, the Hungarian nation spills into western Rumania, and the Rumanian nation spills into the Soviet republic of Moldova. In parts of eastern Europe, elderly people can recall living in several different countries without ever leaving their home villages as war and conquest played havoc with state boundaries. And then there are other groups — Kurds and Palestinians come to mind — that find themselves stateless because of connivance or neglect when borders were being drawn. Since nobody has found a practical way of redrawing existing boundaries to divide the world into thousands of neatly defined nation-states, examples of plurinational states will be around a while longer, whether they be simple binational states such as Belgium or more complex entities such as India.

The United States is a particularly interesting case with special relevance for Canada. Despite the great heterogeneity of its population, it has managed to forge a common identity and outlook that make it a good candidate for the nation-state label. It should be noted, however, that the United States has become a nation-state (or near-nation-state) by continually using state power, sometimes coercively, to create this common national identity. The policy has largely achieved its goals, but at considerable human cost. Furthermore, the process is never complete, especially since immigrants continue to come to the United States (now largely from Asia and Latin America). Whether it will continue to operate as successfully in an era of disintegrating nation-states, transborder identities and growing local consciousness is an open question. Voters in several states, alarmed by the rising use of Spanish in their burgeoning immigrant communities, have felt a need to support resolutions declaring English the sole official language. Other non-English-speaking groups in the past — most notably German-Americans in the nineteenth century — have maintained their language over long periods of time and built impressive institutional networks before finally succumbing to the forces of cultural assimilation. But the great American melting pot has never before faced a single group quite as large as the Mexican immigrants who seem gradually to be reclaiming the Texan and Californian territories stolen from their forebears in the 1840s.

Canada is a less likely candidate than the United States for the nation-state label. While hesitating to break from the ten-provinces mould of constitutional thinking and constantly searching for something its people all hold in common, it has not imposed a unitary national identity on its people as aggressively as its southern neighbour. It acknowledges its two founding peoples and has not quite figured out where natives and newer cultural minorities fit in. Quebec, being more homogeneous than Canada as a whole, comes a bit closer to being a potential nation-state; nevertheless, one sixth of its people have mother tongues other than French, and its native peoples represent a daunting challenge to a unitary conception of nationhood.

It is not uncommon for plurinational states to find autonomist movements chipping away at their authority from within while pressure to join their neighbours in trade groupings chips away at their sovereignty from without. Both these tendencies, one secessionist and the other integrationist, seem well poised to strike during the 1990s. At first glance they appear contradictory. One breaks the state into smaller units and the other subsumes it to larger ones. But this contradiction may be more apparent than real. Leaders of the Scots nationalist movement see no contradiction: they favour the tide towards European integration because it lessens the power that London has long held over their lives, shifting part of it to Brussels instead. As one of many minorities in a Europe of minorities, Scots will be less bothered by English domination of United Kingdom affairs.

In similar vein, prominent Quebec nationalists have been among the most enthusiastic supporters of the Canada-United States Free Trade Agreement. It loosens their dependence on the dominant Ontarians and weakens the arguments of those who say an independent Quebec would be cast adrift economically. The agreement means Quebec could exercise fuller sovereignty without sacrificing the benefits of a geographically broad market for its goods. Opinion polls also have shown that Quebecers are more likely than other Canadians to favour Mexican entry into the North American free trade zone. Of course, letting Mexico in would dilute Anglophone hegemony in North America. But such a stance also reflects a keenness on the part of many Quebecers to broaden their international contacts, even at a time when other polls have shown higher support for the nationalist cause.

Perhaps the most obvious way to reconcile the conflicting claims of larger and smaller units is through a form of government providing for the division of sovereignty between different levels of authority — in other words, federalism. But along with such related concepts as nation, state and sovereignty, federalism has to be approached in a new and broader way. One politician who began to take such a fresh look at federalism is Gil Rémillard, Premier Robert Bourassa's minister of justice, minister of Canadian intergovernmental affairs and key constitutional adviser. In a speech delivered on May 14, 1990, in Aix-en-Provence in southern France, Rémillard said it was unfortunate that the concepts of nation and nation-state have been so closely linked:

> It must be well understood that the fact that Quebecers form a nation in no way obliges them to form an independent state .... The nation-state concept

that came out of the French revolutionary era does
not at all signify that to each nation there must necessarily correspond a state, any more than that to
each state there must correspond a single nation ....
A state ... can exist under a system of shared
sovereignty just as a nation can exist without corre-
sponding to a sovereign state.

Rémillard described federalism, ideally, as a fluid process
that aims for a balance between centralist and autonomist
forces, making it capable of meeting the twin challenges of
nationalist upsurge and economic integration. Federalist
thinking enables the highly centralized Spanish state to grant
limited local autonomy to Catalans and Basques while at the
same time yielding authority to the European Community.
The emergence of supranational structures such as the
European Community and its nascent imitators in other parts
of the world makes it unnecessary, Rémillard argued, for a
nation or a state to exert full sovereignty:

The next century will be the century of federalism.
As we near the turn of the century we see eloquent
testimony to this .... Federalism is a philosophy
rather than a system, a movement rather than a definition, an association rather than a union. It appears
to be the solution both to the secessionist and to the
integrationist movements that characterize this end-
of-the-century period .... Federalism that is well
adapted to social, political and economic circumstances can be the means par excellence of express-
ing nationalisms while avoiding xenophobia.

Were he to deliver the same message in Quebec, Rémillard
might choose to alter his vocabulary, as federalism is a term
that has fallen into bad odour even among some supporters of
the Quebec Liberal Party. But new forms of federalism, perhaps under different names, could soon emerge both in
Canada and elsewhere. Rémillard in fact mentioned that
"several personalities from the eastern countries have come to
visit us lately to observe the evolution of our federalism. It may

be that our experience can benefit countries that are currently in a period of transition." One wonders how the Canadian experience in May 1990 could be held up as a model of anything, although Rémillard's statement was not quite as comical as the offer made by an External Affairs official around the same time to send Canadian constitutional experts to the Soviet Union to help settle the imbroglio over the Baltic states.

As time goes by, René Lévesque's enigmatic concept of a sovereign Quebec in economic association with Canada no longer appears as far removed from traditional Canadian federalism as it once did. With the passing years, the one-or-the-other option that faced voters in the 1980 Quebec referendum on sovereignty-association has come to seem almost beside the point. The choice no longer appears so stark; many shades of grey are now evident.

Part of the Alice-in-Wonderland character of the continuing constitutional debate derives from a growing suspicion that both federalism and sovereignty-association can now mean almost whatever one wants them to mean. Sovereignty-association in fact resembles a very loose form of federalism, while at the same time Canadian federalism can be seen to contain elements of sovereignty-association. In the wake of the Meech Lake failure, the proposals for a new relationship with Canada that the Quebec government began drafting in 1991 lay somewhere along the continuum between what once seemed two wholly incompatible options. Quebec's Allaire and Bélanger-Campeau reports represent efforts to find a comfortable place on that continuum; on the English side, so does Philip Resnick's proposal of a "Canada-Quebec union," put forward in his latest book.

Premier Bourassa has thoughts of his own on new forms of federalism, and his model is the European Community, which he described in a *Time* magazine interview as "one of the greatest achievements of human history." Following his disgrace at the polls in the 1976 election that brought Lévesque to power, Bourassa chose a period of self-imposed exile in Brussels, where he studied the economic and political institutions of the European Community. A few weeks before the Meech Lake collapse, he spoke vaguely of "new superstructures" for Canada, and in the *Time* interview just after the collapse, he referred to the community's founder, Jean Monnet, as "my political idol" and added that the community "is an interesting and probably appropriate reference" in planning Canada's future.

Commenting on Bourassa's remarks, Lise Bissonnette, the new editor of *Le Devoir*, pointed out that even with its plans for monetary union, a common foreign policy and other elements of deeper integration, the community "remains a collection of strong sovereignties .... Tomorrow is not the eve of the member countries being anything other than states, in the full traditional sense of the term." The community has "a minuscule budget, a little more than fifty billion U.S. dollars for twelve countries, a parliament whose functions are still symbolic, a decision-making apparatus that resembles glorified federal-provincial conferences." Bissonnette accused Bourassa of evoking the European model simply to show the opposition that he had a fallback plan after Meech Lake.

When the Treaty of Rome was signed in 1958 laying out the broad guidelines of the future European Community, its signatories clearly hoped to emulate the economic prosperity and political cohesion of which the United States had become the leading symbol. By removing obstacles to trade, they hoped to build the broad markets and the efficient productive capacity that individual states could not hope to achieve.

They came to the painful recognition that this would mean diluting their national sovereignty in certain areas, a price they felt was worth paying, though they were careful not to give up very much. But the community has been evolving through the years. By the end of 1992, all remaining internal trade barriers are slated to disappear, and the community's political institutions expect to exert greater authority. Even so, key measures will still have to be ratified by national parliaments. This serves as a reminder that the community remains a creature of its component states and not a level of government whose sovereignty is unquestioned.

This is not how federalism has been understood in the United States or Canada, where state or provincial approval of federal measures is not required except when the constitution is being amended. In North America the colonies that joined to create new political entities gave their central governments unfettered authority over a clearly defined range of responsibilities. Thus the central governments were in no sense subordinate to state or provincial governments. In Europe, by contrast, the constituent national governments remain supreme even though they may occasionally agree to broaden the purview of the community's authority.

Could a minireplica of the European Community be made to work in Canada? Could two founding peoples on the verge of divorce agree to forms of association that would provide them with common institutions while each of them became sovereign and independent? Could this or some similar formula allow for a parting of ways that allowed them to pool the assets and debts of the existing federal government rather than endure the disruptive and costly nightmare of dividing them? Could their common institutions include, for instance, the central bank and the diplomatic service, or would the two insist on separate currencies and separate sets of ambassadors, at a time when Europe is moving towards monetary union and a closer coordination of foreign policy? How would a Canadian Community operate in the context of a larger free trade agreement with the United States, or even the United States and Mexico? Would Region North America quickly become the North American Community? Would the U.S. *want* to share European-style federal institutions with its two much smaller partners to the north?

Unlike this hypothetical Canadian Community, the European Community was formed by bringing sovereign states together rather than by dismantling existing countries, so Canada would indeed be moving onto uncharted territory. As we have seen, however, the move towards larger economic units and the emergence of smaller national ones are not such contradictory developments as they might appear. It is entirely possible that a looser form of association would be a more appropriate form of organization for Canada, and indeed for North America, than what prevails at the moment.

We can look at what happened in previous attempts at secession in different parts of the world, but most examples are scarcely edifying. The Confederate states of the U.S. South that seceded to protect their God-given right to keep blacks in subjugation were forcibly reincorporated through the military might of the North. The Ibos of oil-rich Biafra who attempted to secede from Nigeria a century later were literally starved into submission. Pakistan's secession from preindependence India was driven by religious rivalries that have left a trail of acrimony to this day. Pakistan itself broke up when its eastern part seceded to form Bangladesh after a civil war and Indian intervention; East Pakistan had had no geographic contiguity with West Pakistan and little contiguity of any other sort either. By contrast, the dissolution of Norway's union with Sweden in 1905 provides a peaceful parallel that proponents of national independence can point to without hesitation, but such instances are rare. One would like to believe that an eventual Canada-Quebec split will provide another instance, but such an outcome is by no means certain. While serious violence seems unlikely, the split could easily take place in an atmosphere of acrimony and spite, to the lasting disadvantage of both sides.

The 1990s have already begun producing secessionist brush fires that could well leave existing maps out of date. A number of Soviet republics, with Lithuania in the lead, have been looking for the exit door. In its lead editorial on June 23, 1990 (the date the Meech Lake deal expired — a coincidence, no doubt), *The Economist* was not afraid to draw parallels with Canada:

> Canada and the Soviet Union, despite their many differences, have one thing in common: they are countries moulded by conquest, not by consent. In time peoples bound together by conquest within a single country may learn to live voluntarily with each other, but only, it seems, if a national identity emerges that is stronger than their sub-national identities.
>
> History's bequest to Canada is to be the country of the American counter-revolution. English-speaking Canadians are mostly happy with their legacy; it accounts for their Tory-turned-social-democratic form of government, their lack of dogma and their sense of duty. The main concern of most English-speaking Canadians is to distinguish themselves from the culturally assertive Whig-turned-individualist citizens of the United States. For Quebecers

such worries are irrelevant; their wish is to maintain their Frenchness, and to keep at bay all English influences, British, American or Canadian.

In this desire to assert their identity, Quebecers are little different from Lithuanians, Latvians and Estonians, or indeed, any of the other peoples fighting to escape the Soviet Union's embrace. Despite the best efforts of communists over 70-odd years, the Soviet Union is not one glorious socialist country; it is a collection of 15 dissimilar republics, whose inhabitants stretch from Europe into Asia, speak different languages, use different scripts, worship different gods and owe greater allegiance to local heroes than to Lenin, Stalin or Mikhail Sergeevich Gorbachev.

The notion that Canada is a country moulded by force may offend certain sensibilities, but the sight of Canadian soldiers and Mohawks facing each other across barricades in the summer of 1990 has made many Canadians more conscious of the extent to which at least some of Canada's political arrangements are historically based on coercion. Indeed, Canada's record is far from unblemished. First the French and then the British pushed Indians off their ancestral lands; later the British subjugated the French by force of arms, and while Quebec's political elites entered willingly into the 1867 Confederation, the subsequent political arrangements never created an entirely happy marriage.

Of course, most other countries were, at least to some degree and in at least some periods of their history, moulded by force as well. Canada's history looks benign compared to the pattern of conquest, extermination, subversion, bullying and forcible annexation that marked the westward and southward push of the United States. The U.S. would presumably fall into *The Economist*'s category of a heterogeneous country in which a national identity has emerged that is stronger than the existing subnational identities, but as already noted, that identity has been achieved largely through the coercive use of state power. Perhaps one of the things Canadians have to be proudest of in their history is the extent to which state power has *not* been used to forge such an identity; on the other hand, this absence of state coercion is not likely to be of much help as the country faces possible dissolution.

Nationalism, *The Economist* notes, "is an enduring phenomenon, and one that looks more enduring than the map of the world as it is drawn in the late twentieth century .... Fuelled by the fires of self-determination, and made economically self-confident by the prospect of regional co-operation, lots of ... countries look set to break up .... Quebec may still separate from Canada. It is hard to see Kashmir remaining Indian forever. And it should be no surprise if in 50 years the map of Africa looks quite different."

For the moment, the world's interest in geopolitical change has been focused on the collapse of Communist orthodoxy in eastern Europe, a reflection in part of the relative triumph of market economics. But even in western countries, where capitalism has been the rule all along, important shifts have occurred. The cradle-to-grave welfare state, which exists in various forms in Canada and most of western Europe, is the legacy of social democratic ideals. Its popular appeal grew so broad in the 1960s and 1970s that liberal and conservative parties stopped opposing it and started telling voters that it was they rather than the social democrats who were really best able to administer the welfare state.

In the 1980s the tables turned, and social democratic leaders in countries as diverse as Australia and Spain began to argue that it was they rather than the liberals or conservatives who were really best able to run an efficient market economy. All of a sudden, social democrats who used to be able to recite detailed policies on just about anything discovered that they were running out of fresh ideas. Not knowing where to turn, they ended up abandoning the ideological initiative to the conservatives. Now, with the bills coming due for the great economic joyride of the 1980s, there are a growing number of signs that the right is floundering as well. Bob Rae's Ontario government may be an important test of whether social democrats can once again turn the tables and exercise ideological leadership.

The freeing of world trade is inevitably bringing about the weakening of sovereign states — and some that were already weak, such as Canada, may disappear. Such weakening or disappearance will remove some vital checks on the activities of multinational corporations and leave local communities and entire countries more vulnerable to the whims of corporate decision-makers half a world away. When governments become heavily involved in economic decisions, that too can create problems and ultimately can make for lower living standards, but governments in democratic societies at least have to answer to those they rule.

Increasingly, these questions will play themselves out in a world of larger trading blocs, smaller sovereign entities, a redefined nation-state and new concepts of federalism — a world towards which, by force of circumstance, Canada could well find itself leading the way.

8

Omens of a New Politics

As 1989 drew to a close, there were an extraordinary number of land mines strewn across the Mulroney government's path. Some of those mines had been there long before Mulroney took office — the oldest and most deeply embedded being the relation of native peoples to Canadian society. Others, such as the Meech Lake Accord and the Goods and Services Tax, had been laid by the government itself, although these too were attempts to deal with problems that long predated Mulroney. As noted in chapter 1, the first explosion occurred over a relatively minor issue: passenger trains. While the immediate controversy was set in motion by the cuts to Via Rail's subsidy in the government's April 1989 budget, it related to several themes that have run through Canadian politics for years: transportation priorities, the importance of east-west institutions to counter north-south economic ties, and the extent to which government decisions should be determined by the bottom line.

The Final Solution to the Railway Problem

When Brian Mulroney's Conservatives took power in 1984, rail enthusiasts were filled with hope. The defeated Liberals had shown only lukewarm support for passenger trains. At one point, they had chopped about 20 per cent of Via's services, although most of these services were later restored. In response to the cuts, the opposition Conservatives established a working group in 1981. It issued a report stating that "the federal government has the responsibility to look after the upkeep, modernization and expansion of passenger train service in Canada as an important part of our national transport system."

The working group urged the government to "revise the priorities in its present transport budget to give more importance to railway passenger service." The report was signed by Don Mazankowski, who would later become transport minister and deputy prime minister.

Any hopes that Mazankowski would follow through on his own recommendations were soon dashed. The new Tory government delayed, and then cancelled, a proposed order for new double-deck cars for long-distance trains comparable to the Superliners that had helped revive Amtrak service in the United States. Things were allowed to stagnate for several years, until the 1989 announcements of the drastic cuts to take effect in January 1990.

There is nothing truly sacred about Canada's passenger trains system as it has existed until recently, and the wisdom of some of Via's spending decisions is questionable. One could wonder why, for instance, hundreds of millions of dollars went into new maintenance shops across the country, including one in Halifax that was slated to close just a year after opening. One could point to Via's needless layers of management and overstaffing aboard some of its trains. Not even ardent train lovers could argue that Via had made the best possible use of the more than $600 million a year in subsidies it was receiving in the late 1980s. Although ridership rose encouragingly in 1988 and 1989, it remained below the averages set in the early part of the decade. Indeed, if the government had been merely pruning, strengthening what remained so that it could rebuild from a more solid base, there might have been considerable merit in what it did.

But what it decreed, without even calling the public hearings provided for under the law, was presented as a final solution. Transport Minister Benoît Bouchard called an inquiry into passenger transport in Canada only *after* ordering half the passenger rail network chopped and placing Via under the virtual trusteeship of Canadian National. Any revision seemed likely to mean yet further cuts ahead. The only ray of hope was a possible high-speed line connecting Montreal, Ottawa and Toronto — and then only if the private sector was willing to assume the costs and risks.

Once upon a time, the railways were all but omnipotent. For more than half a century after its founding, the Canadian Pacific Railway not only had great influence over the government; it seemed it practically *was* the government. The early railway builders wheedled generous allotments of land and forest and minerals as well as cash grants and loan guarantees in return for laying their ribbons of steel.

Apart from some northern resource lines, Canada's railway network was essentially complete when the First World War ended. Since then the demands of railway companies on the public purse have been on a more modest scale. Their relatively meagre capital spending in recent decades has been financed mostly through retained earnings or borrowings. Smug and complacent, for a long time the railway companies seemed hardly to care that they were being outstripped by other modes of transport that were receiving — and continue to receive — vast capital infusions from the public treasury, although not even the federal Department of Transport admits to knowing how much.

The highway and aviation lobbies have secured tens of billions of dollars for an aggressive expansion of infrastructure. They argue that most of this expenditure is recovered through such revenue sources as fuel taxes and airport user fees. But their figures define total costs rather narrowly and revenues rather broadly, neglecting to take into account, for instance, that railways also pay fuel taxes, not to mention property taxes from which highways, of course, are exempt. If highways and airports were put on the same financial footing as railways, Canada might find itself today only with narrow country roads and patchy airstrips incapable of handling jet aircraft. The fact is that all major modes of transport have benefited from public largesse, whether open and exposed as in Via's case or hidden in myriad provincial and municipal accounts as in the case of roads.

The Canadian Institute of Guided Ground Transport at Queen's University in Kingston has estimated that in the late 1980s the air transport system received annual subsidies of about $1.3 billion and the road network about $6.3 billion. Via's $600 million doesn't look so enormous in this context, although on a per passenger-kilometre basis, Via's subsidy of

25.3 cents is much higher than subsidies for other modes. But this can be interpreted to mean not that Via's subsidy was too high but that its passengers were too few. It is possible to imagine that passengers might have been more numerous, and operating deficits lower, had steady public investment allowed the railways to match some of the advances in speed and convenience achieved by competing modes.

Canada's railways have made their concerns over regulatory change well known. But until recently they were strangely reluctant to call for reforms in the way transport is financed. Or perhaps not so strangely. Canadian Pacific has long been a big player in the trucking industry; until recently it owned a major airline as well. Canadian National is government-owned and has had to muzzle itself to avoid conflicts with its sole shareholder. At Via Rail, president Denis de Belleval was fired soon after making two public speeches in which he made the obvious and long overdue observation that fresh capital investment could produce lower operating losses.

In contrast to the railways' relative voicelessness (which leaves unions and voluntary groups such as Transport 2000 to carry the ball), Ottawa is home to active lobbyists such as the Air Transport Association of Canada and the Roads and Transportation Association of Canada. And most provinces have provincial trucking and automobile associations — not that such influence is truly needed since the provincial transport departments are run by empire-builders who do little other than construct and maintain highways.

At the federal level, Transport Canada could more accurately be called Aviation Canada. Departmental listings in English in the government phone book in Ottawa devote 9.7 pages to Transport Canada. Of this space, rail transport merits only one eighth of a page. So much for Transport Canada's concern with railways. The same government department that has direct operational responsibility for airports, air navigation, air traffic control and other aspects of aviation is also responsible for setting general policy and allocating funds covering other modes of transport. When top officials in Ottawa are asked to weigh the conflicting demands of something they control themselves and something run by railway companies in another city, it is hardly surprising that the transport minister gets advice that favours aviation interests. At about the same time as the Via Rail cuts were announced, new funds were freed to expand airports in Toronto and Hamilton. The National Transportation Agency, chaired by former Tory cabinet minister Erik Nielsen, does devote more attention to railways. But the NTA is primarily a regulatory body, without discretionary spending power.

The cuts at Via may turn out to be just the tip of the iceberg. Both CP and CN have begun to recognize publicly that freight hauling could also find itself in serious difficulty unless the railways can halt their decline in market share. In a letter published in the Toronto *Globe and Mail* on August 28, 1989, G.R. Mackie, a CP Rail vice-president, suggested almost plaintively that both railways and trucking companies have to invest for the future and that they need some indication about which way government policy will lean in the future. "Without a clearer sense of that future, necessary investment is delayed, which serves nobody well," Mackie wrote. "It may be that an all-road transportation system in much of the country is the appropriate direction for Canada. But if we get there by default — by governments simply deciding not to decide — we could have the worst of both worlds: little or no railway presence in the truck-rail competitive market, much increased truck traffic and even greater pressure on highways and their funding."

The round of passenger train cuts that took effect in January 1990 left Canada with a skeletal network. Cuts hit hard in the Maritimes, where capacity was reduced by 57 per cent, and even harder in the west, where it diminished by 79 per cent. A city the size of Calgary lost all regular year-round service and was left only with premium-fare summer tour trains. Even in the densely populated Quebec-Ontario corridor, where several studies have shown that high-speed trains running on dedicated track could be profitable from the first year of operation as they are in France or Japan, Transport Minister Bouchard's knee-jerk reaction was that up-front capital costs of several billion dollars would not be covered by government even in part but would have to be financed commercially. How many people would be driving cars if roads were financed that way?

Prime Minister Mulroney was scornful of the opponents of his passenger train cuts, and especially of their evocation of the symbolic significance of railways for Canada's existence as a country. Did they really think Canada was so weak that it could be threatened by the cancellation of a few trains? In January 1990, the question seemed reasonable. But by June, while the trains had been largely forgotten, perception of the weakness of Canada's political structure had spread from a few railway enthusiasts to a majority of Canadians.

Meech Lake (3): Death without Dignity

Having banked heavily on his reputation as the "Great Negotiator" in his run for the Tory leadership and 24 Sussex Drive in 1983-84, Brian Mulroney had brought about the two great achievements of his first mandate, the Free Trade Agreement and the Meech Lake Accord, through heroic feats of last-minute, high-stakes, high-pressure bargaining. And even as the obstacles to the ratification of Meech Lake grew more and more formidable, no one thought it impossible that he would pull something off one more time. Indeed, as late as April 1990, with Tory unpopularity at unprecedented levels and the country deeply divided and unsure about the future, the faith of the Tory caucus in its leader's ability to turn the situation around was reported to be undimmed. Underlying this confidence was the assumption that Meech Lake would, in the end, be ratified; "if Meech Lake fails," one Mulroney strategist was quoted as saying, "it's a whole new ball game."

But if the ratification or otherwise of the accord was still regarded as a major factor in determining the fate of the prime minister, it had become largely irrelevant to the fate of the country he was attempting to govern. What was at stake was not where Canada was going but how it would get there and, perhaps, how quickly. Supporters of Meech Lake argued, with some justice, that rejection of the deal would lead to an independent Quebec. Opponents countered that the decentralized Canada Meech Lake provided for could not long survive; their arguments too were convincing. Supporters saw future constitutional change as being impossible if Quebec was not brought into the constitution, while opponents saw future constitutional change as being impossible if the rigid amending formula provided for in Meech Lake went into effect. Both arguments were plausible.

Had the Mulroney government handled the final stages of the Meech Lake negotiations more adroitly, it might have secured passage of the accord or at least given a better start to the inevitable next round of constitutional talks by allowing Meech to die with dignity instead of in an atmosphere of confusion and recrimination. But the real importance of the Meech Lake debate was the gaping hole it revealed in the foundations of Canadian statehood, and by the time the first ministers gathered in Ottawa in November 1989 to begin the final stage of the Meech Lake misadventure, there was little the government could do to shore up those foundations.

One facet of the problem had manifested itself in the September election in Quebec. Although the election was fought on the bread-and-butter issues with which Premier Robert Bourassa was most comfortable and resulted in the expected landslide majority for his Liberals, it also produced both a stronger Parti Québécois opposition and an angry protest vote by English Quebecers, who gave four seats to the newly formed Equality Party. The upsurge in support for the PQ meant that instead of disappearing, as many had predicted it would, the party remained the only alternative to the Liberals; it would thus, in the normal operation of a two-party system, once again form a government a few years down the road (no Quebec premier since Maurice Duplessis has won more than two consecutive elections). Polls taken at about the same time showed increasing support for the idea of Quebec independence. "Separatism" was not dead after all.

The November first ministers' conference, ostensibly called to discuss the economy, introduced Clyde Wells, premier of Newfoundland since April, as a major player in the Meech Lake debate. Unlike the accord's other two provincial opponents, Frank McKenna of New Brunswick and Gary Filmon of Manitoba, Wells was a constitutional lawyer, and his opposition was neither a bargaining tool like McKenna's nor purely opportunistic like Filmon's. For Wells (as for Pierre Trudeau), all provinces had to have essentially the same status, and none, Quebec included, could be treated differently. Both in private session and on Canada-wide television, the gap that separated

Wells from Mulroney and the pro-Meech premiers was plain, and the extent and nature of the obstacles that Meech faced in English Canada began to become clear.

But Canadians' attention was quickly diverted from the Wells-Mulroney confrontation in Ottawa to the breaching of the wall in Berlin, and then to Prague, Sofia and Bucharest as the Soviet sphere of influence crumbled with astonishing rapidity in the last weeks of 1989. Events in Canada once again seemed to be a sideshow, even to Canadians. Within Canada, the Mulroney government's remaining support was eroding in the face of Via Rail cuts, high interest rates and the impending goods and services tax. Environment Minister Lucien Bouchard's efforts to develop a "Green Plan" were stalled; the government's promise to introduce a Canada-wide day care program had become a matter for the distant future.

When French-English questions surfaced again in February 1990, it was in a somewhat different context. The provisions of Bill 8, Ontario's French-language services legislation adopted in 1986, had come into effect in November 1989, and a number of townships and villages had declared themselves unilingually English to make known their displeasure. While the controversy over French-language services in Ontario had been going on for years and aroused strong passions on both sides, its ramifications had rarely gone beyond the province. But when Sault Sainte-Marie joined the list of municipalities passing "English-only" resolutions (followed a few days later by Thunder Bay), it suddenly recharged the entire constitutional debate.

Perhaps it was because Sault Sainte-Marie was a city rather than a township or village; perhaps it was because of its French name and history as a French outpost; perhaps it was merely timing. In any case, the Sault Sainte-Marie resolution fed Quebec's sense — never very far from the surface — of being unwanted by English Canada, a sense that would now pervade the last months of the Meech Lake ratification process. For many Quebecers, an old television image of anti-French extremists in eastern Ontario wiping their feet on a Quebec flag now became emblematic of English Canadian attitudes towards them. At the same time, when senior members of the Bourassa government made the obvious point that if Meech

Lake failed they would have to consider other options seriously, they provoked a hostile reaction in English Canada.
Meanwhile, some Quebec Liberals were talking openly about
sovereignty; even the federalists had become separatists.

As of early March, more than half of the eight months left
after the acrimonious November first ministers' meeting had
passed, and Ottawa had done little to reconcile the divergent
positions. Nor had it made a serious effort to "sell" Meech
Lake in English Canada (let alone to explain it), as it had so
aggressively "sold" the free trade deal. In late March, Pierre
Trudeau resumed his campaign against the accord, launching
a book of essays by members of his government in which his
own contribution concluded with a venomous attack on
Meech Lake. On the same day, André Laurendeau's journal
was published in Montreal; its perceptions of the gulf between
Quebec and English Canada at the time of the Bilingualism
and Biculturalism Commission now had prophetic overtones.

Meanwhile, Mulroney and Frank McKenna carried out a
coordinated, carefully timed set of moves, motivated in part
by the prime minister's desire to get Trudeau off the front
pages. McKenna introduced the Meech Lake Accord and a
companion resolution with proposed modifications in the
New Brunswick legislature. Mulroney announced the appoint-
ment of a special House of Commons committee, chaired by
former cabinet minister Jean Charest, to study the New Brunswick proposals and conduct public hearings on them. But this
new round of efforts to salvage Meech Lake did not get off to
an auspicious start. Fearing the kind of isolation that had led
to its defeat at the November 1981 constitutional conference,
Quebec adopted a resolution, supported by both the Liberals
and the PQ, that ruled out changes to Meech Lake. Newfoundland, likewise fearing isolation, went ahead with its resolution
to rescind ratification of the accord. Manitoba also indicated
that New Brunswick's proposed changes were not sufficient
to meet its concerns.

In late April and early May, as the Charest Committee made
its way across the country, attention was once again diverted,
this time to a Mohawk reserve on the Canada-U.S. border
not far from Cornwall, Ontario. A dispute between groups of
Mohawks in Akwesasne erupted into violence that resulted in

two deaths by gunfire, and many Canadians heard for the first time of a Mohawk organization called the Warrior Society. While the immediate cause of the dispute was conflicting views of the propriety of gambling casinos and bingo parlours on the reserve, some Mohawks suggested that underlying the violence was the more fundamental question of Mohawk sovereignty.

Meech Lake returned to the spotlight with the release of the Charest Report on May 18. It attempted to establish common ground by suggesting that Meech should be passed as is but then modified through additional amendments to satisfy the dissenting provinces. Instead, it succeeded only in demonstrating how wide the gulf was, proving unacceptable both to Quebec and to Manitoba and Newfoundland. The crisis deepened with the messy resignation of Lucien Bouchard, whose presence in the cabinet had given some Quebec nationalist credibility to the Mulroney government. It was the end of the *beau risque*. Bouchard, who accused the government of preparing to use the Charest Report as a means of hanging Quebec out to dry, became the leader of a bloc of pro-sovereignty Quebec MPs in the House of Commons.

In this atmosphere, talk that Canada might be disintegrating became commonplace, even in English Canadian establishment circles, and it was heard frequently on the interminable special programs that filled the CBC airwaves. Thus, former Vancouver MP and Tory cabinet minister Pat Carney talked about the "deafness [in Ottawa] to important regional needs that finally makes you realize they're not listening and they're never going to listen and so maybe we should develop a different approach." The Toronto business elite's most articulate representative, Conrad Black, spoke of federalism as being at a "dead end" and said, "I would prefer any of the plausible alternatives to a continuation of the status quo, and by 'any of the plausible alternatives,' I mean a sundering of the country into two or more independent countries or some variation of adherence to the United States. I think the institutions we have now served us well for more than a hundred years, but they do not work and demonstrably have failed." And for former United Nations Ambassador Stephen Lewis, "Maybe it's the real Canada beginning to show itself for the

1990s. Maybe this isn't a very nice country." Lewis, like many others, expressed the view that Canada was "falling apart."

Although Mulroney's constitutional adviser and emissary, Senator Lowell Murray, continued to believe that the parties were too far apart for a meeting to be of much use, the prime minister had to do something, and so he decided to "roll the dice" (an expression he would later have cause to regret) and call the premiers to Ottawa on June 3. Over the preceding months, the first ministers had, at least publicly, shown some signs of understanding the extent of dissatisfaction with the closed-door process by which the Meech Lake Accord had been reached, but now that they were together they proceeded to do it again, meeting day after day in marathon private sessions. Observers began to compare the meeting to a political hostage-taking, with the remaining holdout premiers — Wells of Newfoundland and Filmon of Manitoba — serving as the hostages. The more they met, the more essential it became for the sake of appearances that some sort of agreement be reached. In the end one was, and the first ministers emerged for a sham "public session" of mutual congratulation late in the evening of June 9. It did not escape people's attention that Wells was promising only to bring the agreement back for a referendum or free vote in Newfoundland or that Filmon's approval was subject to what he described as a "cumbersome and difficult" process of public hearings and ratification in Manitoba, but the dominant feeling was that Meech Lake had been saved.

The first blow to that notion was delivered by the prime minister himself, who gave an interview to two Toronto *Globe and Mail* reporters on June 11 in which he said — using his habitual gambling imagery — that he had planned the strategy of solving the Meech Lake impasse through marathon last-minute negotiations weeks in advance. Two of the prime minister's qualities that Canadians find least attractive are his bragging and his manipulation; now he was bragging about being manipulative, and it helped crystallize the anger many people felt about the Meech Lake process and especially about the week of closed-door sessions. The second, and ultimately decisive, blow was the work of a group that had never made a secret of its desire to kill the Meech Lake Accord and had little to lose by doing so. Native leaders in Manitoba, with the backing of natives elsewhere in Canada, began meeting to plan a strategy for blocking the accord in the Manitoba legislature, and a native member of the legislature, Elijah Harper, agreed to carry out their scheme. Harper began using the legislature's rules to delay proceedings, and more than 3,000 people, most of them native, signed up to appear at the promised public hearings.

With the Manitoba legislature getting nowhere and the outcome in Newfoundland still uncertain, Lowell Murray was sent out to Winnipeg on June 18 to offer the natives a royal commission if they gave up their blockade; the natives, who had agreed to listen to Murray but not to negotiate with him, rejected his proposal. While in Winnipeg, Murray expressed a few thoughts on democratic process; he found it "incredible that one MLA can tie up a legislature in knots indefinitely," thought it "quite unnecessary" to let all the people who had signed up to appear at public hearings have their say, and urged Manitoba's party leaders to suspend the rules to force a vote by the June 23 deadline. It was also Murray who fronted the government's last-ditch manoeuvre on June 22, arguing lamely that the deadline could be postponed in Manitoba as long as Clyde Wells cooperated and held a vote in Newfoundland. The purpose of this manoeuvre was not so much to salvage the accord as to shift the blame for its demise from the natives to Wells; the prospect of having Meech Lake be seen to die at the hands of native people was simply too risky. But it failed to achieve even that end. English Canadians have frequently adopted other countries' heroes; now they found one they could call their own in Elijah Harper.

The Summer of Native Discontent

On June 25, two days after the Meech deadline expired and two days after the old-style centralist Jean Chrétien was anointed federal Liberal leader, 200,000 Quebec nationalists paraded through the heart of Montreal in an atmosphere of utmost serenity. It was not at all the ugly scene that might have kept the political cauldrons boiling. While Canada's constitutional problems had not even begun to be settled, at least some of the passions appeared to have died down. For a moment it seemed that if Quebec and Canada couldn't stay together, they might be headed for an amicable divorce. The kind of scenario envisioned by Quebec economist Georges Mathews in his book *Comment Robert Bourassa fera l'indépendance*, where Quebec and English Canada, each recognizing its own best interests, agree to reconstitute the country as a European-style "New Canadian Community," did not seem out of the question.

The calm lasted less than three weeks. Native Canadians, having brought down the Meech Lake Accord, were now determined to maintain a prominent place on the post-Meech agenda. The vehicle that ensured that they would not be forgotten was a dispute over a piece of land that soon turned into what neither the free trade debate nor the constitutional crisis had ever been: a military confrontation.

As the Meech debate had amply demonstrated, the great majority of Quebecers, independentists and federalists alike, cling to the idea that Quebec forms a distinct society, and many had difficulty accepting the notion that Mohawks and other native groups might also see themselves as distinct societies with an urge for greater sovereignty. This contradiction, along with the inevitable language frictions, gave added significance to a series of events that happen to have occurred in Quebec but could have erupted in almost any part of Canada.

The events at Kanesatake, near Oka, and Kahnawake were treated as big news partly because they took place near a large metropolitan area. The Lubicon Cree of northern Alberta, who had been locked in struggle for years as oil companies encroached on their hunting grounds, had also built blockades to bolster their claims, but they had access to nothing as strategic as the Mercier Bridge, a lifeline to tens of thousands of carbound Montreal commuters that crosses the Kahnawake reserve near Châteauguay. Awed by the speed of government reaction to the Mohawk tactics, natives in northwestern Ontario and central British Columbia briefly blockaded railway lines passing through their reserves, but since they could not draw upon the political clout wielded by angry suburban motorists, their actions went relatively unheeded.

These events did not occur in a vacuum. They might never have taken on the proportions they did if the federal government had shown greater eagerness to advance the resolution of land claims. Fortunately for authorities at all levels of government, natives in Canada have been slow to anger, but their patience does have its limits. The obtuseness of the golf-course-obsessed Oka municipal council in seeking to raze a stand of pines held as a sacred burial ground by the Kanesatake Mohawks was simply the latest of several provocations. In 1989 the Sûreté du Québec, investigating reports that a native-run bingo game offered prizes exceeding the maximum allowed by provincial law, had raided the Kanesatake band office, if "raid" is an adequate term to designate an action in which all filing cabinets and desks were emptied and their contents seized. And in 1988 the RCMP had raided the Kahnawake reserve (which has close links with Kanesatake) and seized a large quantity of cigarettes on which no Canadian tax had been paid, raising delicate questions of sovereignty (and of a double standard in the pursuit of alleged tax evaders).

Even so, the situation might have evolved more quietly were it not for the fact that the Mohawk nation straddles the boundary between the United States and Canada. Mohawk communities exist on both sides of the border, and many Mohawks who are legal residents of Canada work in the U.S. for several months each year; old treaty rights allow them to cross the border freely. Recruiters for the U.S. armed forces operate even on the Canadian side of the border, and Mohawks, whether residents of the U.S. or of Canada, receive the same training as other recruits in weapons and military tactics. So it was that U.S. military training and U.S.-obtained weapons were put to use in the defence of Mohawk barricades at Oka and Kahnawake. When the Sûreté du Québec violently attacked the barricades and a policeman was shot, the situation became uglier. Bourassa now had little choice but to invite the Canadian army in while he waited for negotiations to advance. Alluding to the messy fights between the SQ and impatient white mobs, replete with clubbing and tear-gassing, *The Economist* of London remarked: "This is not the way Canadians like to think their country is run."

Not that uninterrupted peace has reigned on the Mohawk side; indeed, Mohawk problems of governance take a variety of forms. Thus, the elected band councils imposed by the federal

Indian Act have never fully displaced the moral authority exerted by the traditional chiefs; the inevitable splits have led, among other things, to creation of the Warrior Society, which claims to support the longhouse tradition. In more recent times the Warriors have come to be linked with casino gambling on the American side and cigarette smuggling on the Canadian side, and during a violent series of events on the border-straddling Akwesasne reserve in the spring of 1990, they were often accused of using physical intimidation against their opponents. But nothing works quite as well as outside force at making them look like heroes, a lesson certain police forces have been slow to learn.

Some difficult questions arise. Should natives be allowed to sell untaxed cigarettes or operate high-stakes bingo on their reserves? Should secret societies such as the Warriors be permitted to operate militias and act in defiance of elected band councils? When the issue of native sovereignty is raised, what does this mean in terms of autonomy? We shall not attempt here to provide comprehensive answers. What we can say is that natives formed a mosaic of sovereign nations in North America long before the first Europeans arrived, and they cannot be ignored while Canada wrestles with its internal sovereign relations. Their existence implies at the very least some devolution of authority and the creation of higher units of native self-government to exercise autonomy in certain fields of jurisdiction. Some Mohawks wince at the notion of cigarettes and gambling as economic mainstays but defend the rights of others, as members of a nation they say never renounced its sovereignty, to engage in activities that may happen to be restricted outside their reserves. The question of who decides is far from settled.

The use of loaded terms such as nation and sovereignty has frightened some Canadians away from the concept of native self-government because they equate it with secessionism or with the dreaded notion of special status. Even some advocates of native self-government have only a fuzzy idea of what it means in practical terms, and the new Ontario premier, Bob Rae, who promised almost immediately on taking office in 1990 to work towards native self-government, may end up proving this point despite his good intentions. In remarks that went virtually unnoticed at the time, Quebec cabinet minister John Ciaccia pledged some months before the Oka crisis erupted to work towards "self-government, self-determination, whatever you want to call it" for the Mohawk "nation," a term he did not seek to avoid. In an October 1990 cabinet shuffle, Ciaccia was dropped from the native affairs post, perhaps because he understood the issues too clearly.

Quebec emerged from the unhappy summer of 1990 with a black eye, and not just because of the foolish behaviour of the provincial police. Events beyond the barricades revealed some chilling examples of racist behaviour. A Vancouver photographer of Mexican descent, mistaken for a Mohawk, was roughed up and his film destroyed. The Catholic school board in Châteauguay kept Mohawk pupils out of class for the first two weeks of the school term with no legal justification. A group of Mohawks was forcibly prevented from ferrying food across the St. Lawrence River from Dorval to Kahnawake. Several radio stations boycotted the songs of the popular Montagnais duo Kashtin after a few listeners said they wanted to hear no Indian music. Similar tales abound. Distrust of Mohawks is inculcated from the start of school history classes in Quebec: while the Hurons were French allies in early colonial days, the Mohawks were allied with the British and have not yet been forgiven. (The Mohawks have traditionally been portrayed as villains even in the versions of Canadian history taught in English Canada, but their disputes with New France don't carry quite the same emotional weight as they do in Quebec.)

But to suggest that the Quebec government and Quebecers generally have been comparatively reactionary in their dealings with natives is to underestimate the latent racism in other Canadians. Armed Warriors have never blockaded the Lion's Gate Bridge or the Burlington Skyway, but if they did the reaction would not likely be different. In that sense, there are reasons to be suspicious of at least some of the sympathy the Mohawks gained in English Canada, and there may be some substance to claims by various Quebec observers (including the head of the SQ) that supporting the Mohawks was simply an acceptable way for English Canadians to express their distaste for Quebec. Israelis harbour similar suspicions of non-Jews who criticize Israel or support the Palestinian cause, suggesting that these positions are motivated by antisemitism, and these suspicions are often justified. On the other hand, there are other powerful reasons besides antisemitism to criticize Israel, and so too are there other powerful reasons besides hatred of Quebec to criticize its treatment of natives in general and its handling of the Oka dispute in particular.

We may mention here, however, that income disparities between natives and nonnatives in Quebec fall well below the Canadian average and that few natives languish in Quebec prisons, far fewer than their proportion of Quebec's population would suggest. While the James Bay and Northern Quebec Agreement of 1975 emerged only after court action forced a recalcitrant government to take native land claims into account in its hydroelectric development schemes, it did broaden Cree and Inuit self-determination in the areas of education, health, policing and wildlife management. More recently, natives have contested the new phase of the James Bay hydro project and have been able to base their challenge on terms contained in the landmark 1975 agreement. But the fact remains that natives have scarcely any influence over political decisions in Quebec — perhaps even less than in other areas of Canada where there are significant native populations.

Nor did Ottawa distinguish itself as a source of constructive action during the Oka siege. Perhaps Brian Mulroney was feeling vindictive after Elijah Harper pulled the plug on Meech Lake in the Manitoba legislature. Or perhaps he thought he could get the Quebec government to take most of the political heat, a goal that was largely achieved. Or maybe he imagined he could get away with stalling native claims just as previous governments had done. Whatever the case, the government's image was not helped by the ineptitude of Indian Affairs Minister Tom Siddon. Ottawa, it is true, did come up with the cash to save the Kanesatake forest from the golfers, and just before the final chaotic moments of the standoff, Mulroney's office did issue a promise (though it was bereft of details) to process land claims more quickly and to improve living conditions on Indian reserves.

The dismal conditions on some reserves were dramatized by the visits of two South Africans of very different political stripes, first by then-ambassador Glenn Babb, who was pleased to draw parallels with his country's apartheid system, and later by Anglican Archbishop Desmond Tutu, who appealed for change. While hardly anyone would quibble with the aims outlined in Mulroney's new policy agenda, not everyone took him at his word. Lou Demerais, administrator of the Union of B.C. Indian Chiefs, noted that the quiet discussion Mulroney said his government had been holding with native leaders during the previous year was "so quiet, in fact, that we can't find a single leader who is even aware that such discussion took place."

The signs of goodwill from Ottawa are not at all encouraging if one looks to recent dealings with Alberta's Lubicon Cree as a precedent. After years of struggle to have land set aside as a reserve and after overcoming the earlier opposition of Premier Don Getty, the Lubicon band appeared to be on the verge of a settlement. But then in August 1989 the Indian Affairs department officially approved the creation of a previously unknown entity called the Woodland Cree band, whose leaders had earlier plotted against Lubicon chief Bernard Ominayak. The Woodland band's sole purpose seemed to be to undermine the Lubicon, and its overlapping claims seemed to be getting priority.

CBC Radio's Royal Canadian Air Farce was not far from the mark with its story about an operative with the Canadian Security Intelligence Service who was famed as a master of duplicity and deception; a colleague remarked that Indian Affairs had been sorry to lose him. In November 1990 the Canadian Human Rights Commission recommended the outright abolition of the department, along with the Indian Act it administers. But no such proposal will ever have native support if it turns out to be a stratagem (as was the highly unpopular 1969 white paper) to integrate natives into the general population.

The signing of the Free Trade Agreement gravely weakened one of the underpinnings of Canada's existence as a country: the maintenance of east-west economic ties. The Meech Lake misadventure exposed the weakness of a second one, the agreement to live together (or shared misunderstanding) between English and French Canadians. And the Oka standoff challenged yet a third: the existence of a native population whose agenda could be indefinitely postponed and generally ignored whenever serious politics was being discussed. By the time the barricades came down in Oka in September, the weakness of Canada's state structure was manifesting itself in other areas as well. The collapse of the old assumptions had begun to have ramifications in the electoral arena, notably in a convincing win by Lucien Bouchard's Bloc Québécois in an August byelection in a traditionally Liberal Montreal seat and in the upset victory by the NDP in September's provincial election in Ontario. And the federal Tories were insulated from immediate catastrophe only by the circumstance that they didn't have to face the electorate again for another two years.

The NDP: From Conscience to Government

As he looks toward the next federal election, Brian Mulroney faces a more disquieting prospect than any prime minister since Mackenzie King in the latter days of the Second World War. The issues are identified — the omnious recession, the constitutional impasse, free trade, high interest rates, native resentment, the GST. And the unfortunate David Peterson's characterization of the public as "cranky" has been one of the milder expressions used to describe the mood of the body politic.

But it is not only the apparent political destiny of the Progressive Conservative Party that represents a disquieting prospect. Some people are prepared to dismiss the Bloc Québécois as a byelection wonder, while others see the current upsurge of the Reform Party (along with the unusually large vote gathered in the Ontario election by such fringe groups as the Family Coalition and Confederation of Regions parties) as a replay of the temporary fractures in the old-line parties represented earlier in the century by the Progressives, Farmer-Labour, Social Credit and the Créditistes. They may be right. But it is also possible that we are witnessing something quite different: the end of the exclusive dominance of the Liberal and Conservative parties.

Thus, Bob Rae's Ontario election victory signals the likely emergence of the NDP as the largest single party in English

Canada. But that does not mean either a widespread endorsement of what the NDP has traditionally stood for or the development of an alliance of groups and regions that can constitute a stable majority at the federal level. Rather, with the NDP electing strong contingents in Ontario and the west, the Liberals concentrated in Ontario and the Atlantic provinces, the Reform Party taking a significant number of western seats and Quebec split between the Conservatives and the Bloc Québécois — and with no party winning as many as, say, a hundred seats — the stage would be set for a politics of permanent deadlock and fragmentation. This would not be minority government in the sense that we have known it under Diefenbaker, Pearson, Trudeau and Clark at the federal level or under Bill Davis, David Peterson and Gary Filmon provincially. It would be a kind of government for which we would have to look more to countries such as Italy, Israel and India for models than to anything we are familiar with in Canada.

The essential problem is that few if any of the Mulroney government's acts of omission and commission that have won it its present unpopularity constitute either a break with the past or even a significant change in course. The issue is simply this: during Brian Mulroney's shift many of the bills came due — after all, the policies that led to the current situation have essentially been bipartisan ones. Most Canadians realize this. Thus the Liberals are mired in the same rut as the Conservatives because they would probably have paid the bills with the same currency for our lack of coherent economic policies, our attempts to deal with the problems of Canada-U.S. integration by seeking still more integration, and our avoidance of the structural problems of Canadian federalism. And Canadians seem to realize this also.

Nothing in Jean Chrétien's tenure as Liberal leader suggests that he has found a new direction for himself, his party, or the country. While he never hesitated to issue a ringing denunciation of the Meech Lake Accord or the GST, he did everything possible to avoid committing himself to alternative courses of action. In the last weeks of the Meech Lake ratification period, which also happened to be the last weeks of the Liberal leadership campaign, he retreated to complete public silence — all the while trying to find a solution behind the scenes so that he wouldn't have to assume the leadership at the moment of Meech Lake's collapse. And in September, speaking to the stunned Ontario Liberals a week after their election defeat, he said the election meant that "people are so fed up with [Mulroney's] government that they were ready to get tough with government in general." Consistent with that political *non sequitur*, Chrétien still refused to enunciate a single policy. Even though two years before an election discretion is always the better part of valour, the image persists of a Liberal Party not in a policy vacuum but rather with a political mindset remarkably similar to that of the Conservatives. In Ontario, David Peterson ended up looking like Brian Mulroney, and the voters noticed the resemblance.

In that sense, the NDP's main asset in the Ontario election was that it was not the Liberals or the Conservatives. Like many other radical parties that have suddenly found themselves holding the reins of government, the Ontario NDP came to power largely because the voters had tried everything else. But the at least partly accidental character of the NDP's victory (and the fact that it was achieved with less than 40 per cent of the popular vote) should not obscure the historic nature of the shift in Canadian politics it represents.

In postwar Canada, the Liberals would note the popularity of various social measures proposed by the CCF and would halfheartedly adopt them, or parts of them. In the words of Lynn McDonald in *The Party That Changed Canada*, longtime CCF leader M.J. Coldwell would "set out comprehensive strategies for reform, yet support whatever halfway measures the government would accept. As leader in the postwar period, Coldwell had the unhappy experience of helplessly watching the Liberals theft of his party's policies." CCFers were victimized both ways. They saw their votes drifting away to the Liberals on one hand while they were castigated as dangerous radicals on the other. They were taunted from the government benches as "Liberals in a hurry"; in the same vein, Marc Lalonde more recently characterized the CCF's successor, the New Democratic Party, as being Liberals with principles.

Being the conscience of a government that had to do unconscionable things had its consolations, especially when the Liberals were in a minority position. Thus the Pearson minority government, despite its mistakes, left a record of valuable social legislation, and when NDP leader David Lewis was able to keep the Trudeau Liberals' feet to the fire between 1972 and 1974, we got pension increases, indexing, family allowance increases, the creation of Petro-Canada and the Foreign Investment Review Agency, and a host of other measures. Even if a perverse public not only failed to appreciate its benefactors but also seemed to enjoy humiliating them at election time, the party learned to make do and even love the reward virtue usually receives. As Stephen Lewis, the party's most articulate spokesperson, has suggested, "The beauty of the party is the strength of its principles .... As long as we have a democratic socialist left to influence policy, that's enough. You don't need to exercise power."

This comforting notion means one's principles can remain intact as long as they never have to be acted on. Thus, one could balance the meagre political rewards for virtue against the blameless life of the loyal opposition. Exercising power was not only unnecessary: it was to be avoided all all costs. This abhorrence of office extended even to the notion of shared power. When Bob Rae toyed with the idea of a coalition during negotiations with the minority Ontario Liberals in 1985, it was rejected by the party elders, and when Pierre Trudeau proposed NDP participation in the govenment in 1980, Ed Broadbent didn't even discuss it in caucus.

The rejection of power presented the NDP with another luxury. It could forever play with high-sounding but irrelevant economic strategies. Typical hobbyhorses include "industrial democracy," "cooperation strategies" and vague notions of corporatism. Ed Broadbent liked to remind listeners that the president of Volvo was a social democrat and that he looked forward to the day when the president of GM would be a fellow traveller with the NDP. He overlooked the fact that GM Canada is a branch-plant operation and that its president is a middle-level manager on a brief assignment. The industrial or any other policy of GM is not determined in Canada.

With such material the NDP can avoid the sticky areas of nationalization and economic control. New Democrats note with relief and pride that every public opinion survey indicates that Canadians will trust them with anything but the economy. Thus, during the last federal election, Ed Broadbent concentrated on speculative peripheral issues while cheerfully handing John Turner the central economic issue of free trade.

This stance also frees the NDP from either rejecting or accepting the sometimes artless praise it often receives for its perceived new maturity. A typical example was provided by Geoffrey Stevens before the last federal election. According to Stevens, the NDP is now "a mainline bourgeois political party which can vote to break a strike of west-coast grain handlers, a non-militaristic party which can contemplate with equanimity increased defence spending, a reform party which can envisage governing without performing radical surgery on existing social and economic institutions." To paraphrase another social democrat, Mackenzie King, social democracy if necessary but not necessarily social democracy.

And so Ed Broadbent contemplated the bizarre performance of John Turner during the early stages of the 1988 federal election and the Liberal free fall and pronounced himself satisfied that the NDP would replace the Liberal Party. It would be the best of all possible worlds: the NDP would be the opposition. But what Broadbent was really talking about was not so much *replacing* the Liberals as *succeeding* them — in other words, becoming Liberals. If the NDP were to replace the Liberals, it would mean that politics would become more polarized (or at least different), and the Liberal constituency would dissolve. And for this to happen, the NDP would have to accentuate its differences with the old politics, not fudge them as suggested by Geoffrey Stevens.

While it is far too early to speak of the once-dominant Liberals in the past tense, it does appear that they may well be the victims of the nineties and that the NDP may at long last replace — or succeed — them. Nor will this necessarily be a transplant of the political polarization that developed after the decay of Whig England, because the issues on the political agenda in Canada are much broader than those of class distinctions and internal class relationships. Indeed, examining the makeup of what we euphemistically call the Canadian business community, we could conclude that as Canada enters the new century there are two nations — one privileged, the other powerless — in the same sense that there were in

England as the twentieth century dawned, except that in our case one nation lives elsewhere. Our issues, in the broadest sense, are all-encompassing. They include the establishment of a new relationship, if any is possible, between English and French Canada; the environment; aboriginal claims; and political survival — again if that is possible — in the context of North American economic integration.

In this respect, it is interesting to examine the composition of the new NDP government in Ontario and the first tentative steps the government has taken since its election.

Many political lifetimes ago, when Brian Mulroney was trying to nominate a full list of Quebec Progressive Conservatives to contest the 1984 federal election, he confronted a difficult problem. The party at that time existed mainly in the imagination. And while there were enough ambitious friends and political pros around to nominate in every constituency, not many of them were enthusiastic about going down to what seemed to be inevitable defeat. As a result, Mulroney had to fill out his list with some political unknowns and second-string *indépendantistes* — who have now turned out to be his last line of defence.

Bob Rae confronted a similar situation as he filled out the lists in Ontario in 1990. There were many prominent members of the NDP around Ontario prior to the election victory. But many who had been through the election meat-grinder before were simply unprepared to be fodder again. In addition, an unusual number of sitting NDP members were so little enamoured of their chances of reelection that they bailed out before the writs were issued. Robin Sears, who had gone from being one of Ed Broadbent's advisers to running the Bob Rae operation, went to work for the Liberal government. As David Peterson slowly began his election waltz, many NDP constituency organizations began the thankless task of finding someone to do another thankless task.

Forced by circumstance to move away from the party's traditional candidate pool, Rae found potential nominees in the grassroots and the periphery. This has already caused some problems, but taking the caucus as a whole, adversity or necessity has allowed the party to take advantage of its broadening base. As a movement or conscience, the party has over the last few years attracted activists not only from the trade union movement but also from just about every other people's organization in existence — feminists, the peace movement, environmental groups, food banks, tenants' associations. And fortune has now thrust many of these people into the Ontario legislature and cabinet. The government may be light on lawyers, business executives and even labour executives, but there are nurses, teachers and workers. Indeed, circumstance has made the new NDP government in Ontario probably the most broadly based coalition in history. This will create problems in several directions as inexperience navigates between expectations and real politics. Yet for all that the government seems by composition one that at least approaches an answer to the frustration of voters who feel alienated and excluded from the political process.

Again by circumstance, this represents a new approach to a problem that the NDP has struggled with since its founding, as did the CCF before it. It has always been one of the goals of the party to represent the disenfranchised, even when the disenfranchised weren't interested. This goal was initially expressed in terms of "farmer-labour unity," then as the "political arm of labour," and then through direct affiliation, which was to give muscle and depth to the new NDP that the old CCF never enjoyed. By any measure, except possibly financial, this has not happened. Moreover, the labour affiliation appears to be connected to the dismal ratings the public gives the NDP on economic issues. Nothing seems to work. The relationship between the trade union movement and the party has been particularly rocky. In the first place there has been a fundamental misapprehension of the labour movement and its political alliances and clout; although for a time the leadership of some especially American-oriented internationals did force a rightist, continentalist position (which incidentally gave the social democratic vote in Quebec to the Parti Québécois by default). We speak of "big labour" and its political control of the NDP. There is no "big labour" in Canada. By western industrial standards, trade union membership in Canada is low. Furthermore, fewer than half of unionized workers are members of the Canadian Labour Congress, and of this number only about 8 per cent are directly affiliated with the NDP.

If we approach this from another angle, however, the NDP in alliance with the trade union movement represents a cogent political force. Its strength lies in its ability not only to speak to the economic interests of workers but also to make common cause with other groups such as the environmental, peace and feminist movements. This ability adds considerably to the potential breadth and attractiveness of the NDP as these groups enter directly into politics. No party whose traditional base is in the corporate world has the same potential, especially at a time when business interests are identified solely with the bottom line and the bottom line has pretty well abandoned Canada.

In this sense, the restructuring of Canadian politics will involve a restructuring of our political parties, from which the NDP may be in the best position to benefit. As traditional politics has played itself out in Canada, the NDP, like the CCF before it, has had its federal hopes constantly dashed on the shoals of indifference in Quebec and was thus seen as improbable in Ontario. Should Quebec become independent, of course, the Liberals and Conservatives will be hurt far more than the NDP.

Already, The NDP's powerful provincial wings in Ontario, Saskatchewan and British Columbia have their own constitutional agendas, and they are not necessarily compatible with one another. This makes it difficult for the federal party to develop a constitutional position of its own. But the fact remains that relations among the different regions of Canada will now be brokered through the NDP as they were once brokered through the Liberal Party. As the recognition grows that the old politics cannot address any of the real political, social and economic issues that confront the country, the biggest surprise coming out of the September 1990 Ontario election could be not so much the result itself as the new politics towards which it points.

In the fall of 1990, the shape of any such new politics remained a blur on a distant (or perhaps not so distant) horizon. The shape of the old politics, on the other hand, was all too clear, and came into focus once again as the government's amendments to the Excise Tax Act giving force to the new Goods and Services Tax, having passed the House of Commons, made their way towards the Senate.

9

The East Germany of North America?

As the battle in the Senate over the Goods and Services Tax gathered force in the fall of 1990, the Mulroney government resorted to a time-honoured argument. The GST had been passed by the House of Commons, which consisted of elected representatives of the people of Canada. The unelected Senate had no right to overturn the democratic decision of the elected House. This view of the relationship between the House and the Senate had long been the prevailing one, and it meant that the Senate never really used the broad powers allocated to it under the constitution. Because of Canada's continuing constitutional paralysis, the country had never managed to abolish the Senate, redefine its powers or reform its method of selection.

And yet in late 1990 the argument about the illegitimacy of the unelected Senate fell on deaf ears. For even if in the minds of most Canadians the claim of the Senate to legitimacy might be weak, the claim to legitimacy of the House of Commons, and of the government that is supposed to be responsible to it, was not much stronger. The question had gone beyond whether the Mulroney government was a good government or a bad government; people now questioned whether it was entitled to govern at all. One manifestation of this lack of legitimacy has been the government's repeated failure to "gain control of the agenda." It has neither the financial resources nor the political capital to do more than react — and inadequately at that — to initiatives that originate elsewhere.

The reasons for the erosion of the legitimacy of both the federal government and Parliament have partly to do with the actions of the Mulroney government itself. After all, the government that tried to uphold the dignity of the House of Commons in the battle over the GST was the same government that a few months earlier had committed Canadian troops on two different fronts (Oka and the Persian Gulf) without seeing any need to consult the House. Furthermore, the Mulroney Tories' bottom-line approach to government has eaten away at the rationale for the very existence of a federal government in Canada. As we noted in 1988 in *Selling Out*, this approach represented not so much an about-face from the policies of previous governments as a change in emphasis. This change was accentuated in 1989 after the Tories' reelection and the signing of the Free Trade Agreement when deficit reduction became the government's primary stated goal. As we saw in the case of Via Rail, the emphasis on the bottom line has done extensive damage to institutions that have fostered whatever fragile sense of connectedness and common experience Canadians have shared.

The effects of this approach could be seen again in late 1990 when the CBC closed television stations in a number of smaller cities across Canada. As usual, there were arguments about whether the stations represented the best possible use of scarce federal money, but these arguments missed a crucial point. If passenger trains have a significance for the existence of Canada as a country beyond the people who actually ride them, so too do Canadian television stations have a significance beyond the people who actually watch them. At one time, deficit or no deficit, the Mulroney government had considered nuclear submarines essential to maintaining Canadian sovereignty in the Arctic. A far stronger case could be made that a local television newscast (at a fraction of the cost) is essential to maintaining Canadian sovereignty in Windsor.

But the crumbling of the legitimacy of the federal state goes far beyond the actions of a single government. There were always contradictions and misunderstandings at the core of Canada's existence as a country, and after 1945 both its gathering constitutional crisis and its increasing absorption into the American orbit helped bring those contradictions and misunderstandings to the surface. The relatively vigorous measures taken by the Trudeau government to promote what it saw as the "national interest" (a concept alien to the Mulroney Tories), whether in the form of a bilingual civil service, the War Measures Act or the National Energy Program, helped mask that process for a while, but it took hold again with a vengeance once Trudeau was gone.

The logic of Canada's existence as a country has been undermined gradually, over a long period of time. But we have argued that the signing of the Free Trade Agreement represented a watershed in this process. On both a real and a symbolic level, what the various regions of Canada share with one another that they don't also share with the United States has been reduced. It is partly because Canadian sovereignty is so tenuous that the claims of both Quebec and the native people to sovereignty come through so strongly. As the extent to which Ottawa is a centre of economic decision-making falls off under the influence of both the Free Trade Agreement and Canada's foreign debt, the advantages to be gained from being part of the Canadian federation diminish correspondingly.

We are living in some respects in the East Germany of North America. Of course there are differences, and events will unfold differently. Canadians are not lining up at the border in consequential numbers to leave. And yet in terms of state structure, Canada is no more sound in 1991 than East Germany was in the fall of 1989. The country is facing crises — both on the economic front and on the constitutional front — that it may not be able to withstand. These crises are the result of decisions made over several decades, and in some cases going back much further than that, whose cumulative effect has been to narrow our range of choices severely. To take one example, a necessary condition for dealing with both the economic crisis and the constitutional crisis may be the abrogation of the Free Trade Agreement. But it will be far more difficult to abrogate the agreement than it would have been not to have undertaken free trade negotiations in the first place in 1985.

Still, to say that our range of choices is narrow is not to say that we have no choices at all. It is not our purpose here to put forward a detailed plan for Canada's future. But we would like to suggest three major changes in current Canadian practice that could make it possible for any plan that does emerge to be one that Canadians choose themselves.

The first change has to do with democratic structures, for the Mulroney government's disappearing legitimacy is related to the increasing inadequacy of the "five-year dictatorship" model of representative government. This development has operated with special force after 1988 as events both in Canada and elsewhere have created a dramatically different situation from the one in which the Tories won their second majority. In November 1988, ratification of the Meech Lake Accord appeared likely, indefinite postponement of native demands seemed a viable strategy, a low Canadian dollar made benefits for Canadian exporters from the free trade deal a credible prospect, and an eternal East-West conflict was one of the pillars of the international order. George Woodcock has written:

> The five-year parliamentary term means that for a period long in relation to the rapidity of change and communication in the modern world, the people have no redress against a government that, like Brian Mulroney's today, has become irrevocably unpopular but clings on because — long ago, in terms of contemporary time — it once won a majority. A majority two years ago can be a fiction today.

In this sense, a crucial element in the legitimacy of a government, the consent of the governed, is lacking. "If the people are kept away from the process of governing themselves," Woodcock suggests, "they will take the law into their own hands, and we will see our streets filled with crowds, angry yet nonviolent like those in Eastern European cities that by their persistent return swept arrogant leaders from power."

While the prospect of hundreds of thousands of people in the streets of Toronto or Vancouver may seem remote, Canadians' anger at having no power over decisions that vitally affect them is very real, as has been shown in the debates over both Meech Lake and the GST. Dissipation of this anger will require far more than ill-conceived, poorly constructed expedients for "listening" to Canadians such as the Spicer Commission. Rather, it will require structures that allow people to participate on an ongoing basis in making the decisions that affect them. One program for achieving this end was put forward by the agrarian and labour radical movement in western Canada early in the twentieth century. It centred on legislation by direct citizen initiative, provisions for the recall of elected officials who had lost popular support and wide-spread use of the referendum. This program has continued to have many adherents in the west, and it has been adopted by the latest vehicle of western protest, the Reform Party — al-though it would likely lead to something very different from the right-wing economic and social policies the Reform Party also advocates. In any case, democratic structures along these lines are overdue in Canada, and their absence is compound-ing the difficulty of dealing with our present problems.

A second change has to do with how Canada — and more specifically, English Canada — conceives of itself constitution-ally. The problem can be stated simply. The relationship be-tween Quebec and the rest of Canada has reached the end of its rope. A new one, whether it takes the form of complete separation or renewed federalism or something in between, has to be negotiated. But with whom does Quebec negotiate? The Meech Lake fiasco, arising out of the assumption of ten equal provinces, quite properly discredited the federal-provincial model of constitutional negotiation. The alternative proposed by Quebec — one-on-one negotiation between Quebec and the federal government — is no more promising. After all, the fed-eral government is supposed to be the government of both Quebec and English Canada, so that it is hardly in a position to represent English Canada alone in negotiations with Quebec. Its unsuitability is all the more obvious in a situation where both the prime minister and the leader of the opposition are Quebecers.

English Canada has never conceived of itself as a distinct entity; English Canadians identify with a Canada that includes Quebec, and also with their particular province, region or ethnic group, but not with something in between. And yet the latest set of proposals from Quebec will finally confront Eng-lish Canada with the need to answer the question not so much of what it wants as of what it is.

As René Lévesque often noted, the structure of Canadian government, with its various levels and overlapping juris-dictions, makes this country both overgoverned and poorly governed. And this very structure stands in the way of both French and English development. Part of the attraction of the sovereignty option in Quebec is that it achieves the grand goal of eliminating one level of government. But a case for federalism could be made in both Canadas if it would simply begin by describing our reality. Canada is not composed of ten provinces in which an equal devolution of federal power to Quebec and Prince Edward Island can both satisfy one and be successfully managed by the other. Nor can some special status be developed that would require Quebec to submerge its basic right of self-determination in endless Supreme Court cases. The constitutional impasse can be broken only if Quebec is recognized as a nation. And English Canada can emerge from this process with some hope of continued existence only if it recognizes itself as a nation. Furthermore, both these entities, with their relatively clearly defined territories, share the total land mass with an aboriginal population that, like the other groups, is less interested in assimilation than in self-rule and self-determination. The issue then becomes to find a constitutional and organizational framework to reflect this reality. And this must be done in the context of the Free Trade Agreement, which not only changes the parameters of our politics but also lends a new urgency to the solution of long-festering problems.

It would be rash to try to predict what kind of state structure will emerge out of the rigid, dysfunctional form of federalism that is currently serving Canadians so poorly except to say that it will almost certainly be something very different from what we have now. In their book on the state of Canadian public opinion, *The Big Picture*, Allan Gregg and Michael Posner conjecture that what may be evolving is a much more decentralized Canada:

> Perhaps the most likely scenario is the evolution of a structure similar to Switzerland's: five strong cantons representing separate cultures, governing in the interests of those cultures, with a federal government that is little more than the instrument of their collective commercial interests. Canada as Switzerland? It's only speculation, of course. And given the

state of public opinion as we begin the 1990s, it may even be optimistic.

It is not only public opinion that make such a scenario seem optimistic; it is economics and geopolitics as well. The problem with a decentralized Canada would be that the southward pull would be stronger for most regions than east-west ties; while Switzerland is surrounded by larger neighbours, there is no single dominant power like the United States. There are no Alps and no centuries-old traditions of sturdy independence to protect Canadian distinctiveness. And how would a Canadian government serve the collective commercial interests of Canada's regions when it has signed away much of its capacity to protect those interests in the Free Trade Agreement?

A more promising approach is taken by Philip Resnick in his recent *Toward a Canada-Quebec Union*. Resnick proposes the establishment of a specifically English Canadian government that would operate more or less the way the federal government does now except that it would share some joint institutions with the government of Quebec. Far from eliminating one of the two levels of government, this proposal would create yet a third (although Resnick does suggest ways to minimize the extra bureaucracy involved). But some such structure may well be necessary if the aspirations of both Quebec and English Canada are to be met.

To say that the current constitutional crisis is primarily an English Canadian one is not to suggest that Quebec's path to sovereignty (or whatever status it eventually chooses) will be entirely smooth. One major obstacle across Quebec's path to sovereignty is posed by the competing claims and interests of its native population. The Quebec government would be reluctant to agree to any settlement that gave it anything less than full sovereignty over the entire territory of Quebec. But large portions of that territory are encumbered by outstanding native land claims. Does Ottawa, with its "fiduciary responsibility" for native people, have the right simply to drop these claims in the lap of a sovereign Quebec? Or would a settlement between Quebec and English Canada, if one were possible, also have to include a settlement of questions of native self-government or sovereignty? Such questions, difficult enough under any circumstances, will be that much harder to resolve in the post-Oka mood of mistrust between natives and white Quebecers. Nevertheless, it is in English Canada that the greatest leaps of constitutional imagination will be required.

Finally, Canadians need governments at all levels that are prepared to act in the collective interest. Perhaps a starting point in this process would be to challenge the current assumption that the political and economic processes taking place today are somehow beyond human control. It is a given that the modern state cannot withstand the process of global economic rationalization and decentralization. Thus, Thomas Courchene, director of the School of Policy Studies at Queen's University, has said:

> Given that the FTA embraces markets it is inherently decentralizing, since the markets themselves are inherently decentralizing.... The FTA is decentralizing in yet another sense. The political economy of the east-west transfer system will come under increasing scrutiny in the context of the FTA north-south integration.... What is clear is that our tradition of sheltering various regions of the country from market forces is going to become progressively difficult, both economically and politically.

According to this argument, globalization is an objective process arising out of the workings of the market, which itself is impervious to human influence. The Free Trade Agreement is a mere manifestation of this process, which moves passively yet inexorably to destroy the very underpinnings of "the east-west transfer system" (otherwise known as Canada). And so as successive federal budgets reduce transfer payments to the provinces, concepts embedded in programs such as the National Health Act no longer relate to the modern reality of the market. Before the end of the century the federal government will be contributing nothing to the public health system, and the act will become a dead letter. And it is all so natural: it is simply progress. To oppose this process is not only fiscally irresponsible; it is as futile as calling back the tide.

Conventional wisdom today determines progress and practicality within the context of "the bottom line," an ugly, overused and inexact term that is defined by "experts." Yet life itself often confounds. An example of the confounding of the bottom-liners can be seen in the present impasse in the "Uruguay Round" of GATT discussions. The Europeans insist on maintaining their thirty-year-old policy of price supports, export subsidies and import levies for agricultural products. There are political, social, cultural and even esthetic reasons to maintain a European agricultural system — not to mention such economic considerations as not impoverishing the countryside and filling the cities with the displaced unemployed. Indeed, the movement towards the "New Europe" includes a new social contract that promises not to tear the social traditions and fabric of Europe apart. That is why the movement enjoys popular support. This same social contract, however, affronts the bottom-liners.

The notion that governments do not, should not and cannot intervene massively in the economy is pure mythology. The question is simply how they intervene, and in whose interests. A case in point is the government response to the difficulties faced by Algoma Steel.

If Algoma closes, consultants argue that 23,100 jobs will be affected. The 8,000 jobs lost in Sault Sainte-Marie will represent about 20 per cent of the area's income. The city would lose $75 million in tax revenues over the next three years, Ontario more than $85 million and Ottawa about $185 million. These numbers certainly put into perspective any amounts that will be required to keep Algoma going.

It wasn't long ago that the Canadian steel industry was considered to be efficient and modern with high and increasing productivity. But with the signing of the Free Trade Agreement, Canadian steel exports to the United States declined and imports from the U.S. increased. While tariffs have come down, the complex skein of American antidumping regulations that operate against Canadian exports remains in place. The FTA has also added restrictions on the manner in which governments can intervene in the industry. As a result, the viability of the once-booming Canadian steel industry is now a real question.

When Hamilton-based Dofasco purchased Algoma in 1988 for $560 million, it was regarded by industry experts as a perfect corporate fit. Algoma could supply Dofasco with raw steel and eliminate the time and expense of building a new mill. The debt Algoma carried at the time seemed to create very little difficulty. Dofasco needed the raw steel then, and it needs it today. Indeed, in walking away from Algoma and taking a $713-million writeoff, Dofasco did not claim a tax recovery. It would seem that Dofasco sees itself as part of any restructuring of Algoma and simply wants some government help in paying off its debt.

The suspicion that the bailout being organized is not for Algoma, the Canadian steel industry or the community but for the owners and lenders is supported by history. Public funds are what got Algoma started in the last century when it was hailed as the forerunner of northern economic development. The money that poured into Sault Sainte-Marie all disappeared by 1903, and the company got its first bailout. It came back for more money in the 1930s. And like other large corporations, Algoma was set up to prosper in the postwar era by the largesse of the Canadian taxpayer and the policies of C.D. Howe.

Commenting on Algoma's recent difficulties, Duncan McDowall, the author of *Steel at the Sault*, has described the various financial bailouts at the intersection of public interest and private gain. The public interest in the survival of Algoma is obvious, as he says: "In the long suffering Northern Ontario economy, Algoma is a high-wage Canadian owned and technologically modern generator of activity. Given the right financial auspices, it should be able to produce structural and tube steel profitably for national and export markets." But while arguing for a bailout, McDowall wants it done differently: "Ontario and Ottawa cannot, however, repeat the experiences of 1903 and 1935 — today public purpose must rank ahead of private gain.... Equity participation offers one answer." That of course is the rub. For the government to demand equity in Algoma would mean intervening in the interests of the community rather than those of the owners and would thus be a challenge to historic assumptions about government participation in the economy.

It is also a given that we have become or are on the verge of becoming impoverished because of years of wasteful government spending and that therefore the deficit and debt must be cut. Government cutbacks in social spending, the argument proceeds, are a sad but necessary reaction to a situation our own impulsive greed created. Spending must be cut even though these cuts may be undesirable, unfortunate and even hurtful. Sacrifices must be made to fiscal integrity — some trusts are more sacred than others.

It is not that government spending is challenged — it increases constantly. But just as the tax burden is shifted, so also is the weight of expenditures. Consider for example a current "megaproject," Hibernia, to which the government has committed almost $6 billion in grants and guarantees. It has been estimated that this amount means that it will cost more than $200,000 per job created in Newfoundland. One is reminded of John Maynard Keynes, who — contemplating British subsidies to keep some coal pits open — suggested filling the pits with pound notes and letting the miners dig them out. On a much smaller scale, Michael Walker of the Fraser Institute dissected a contract worth between $800 million and $1 billion that Lavalin, the Quebec engineering firm, negotiated with the Thai government. The project will cost the Canadian government $383 million in loans grants and guarantees.

Anyone who has ever listened to the speeches at a Conservative convention or read any position papers advanced by leadership hopefuls knows quite well that social spending runs counter to the ideology of the Conservative Party, which at one time or another has opposed every social measure ever proposed in Canada. If current financial problems did not provide a rationale for cuts, the government would have invented others. Nor does the notion of affordability ring true in the manner in which it is presented: "Can we really afford medicare, or pensions, or education — all this free stuff that doesn't return a profit?" This question is usually accompanied by one of two caveats: "We would really love to but we must cut our coat to fit our cloth" or "This is a tough competitive world and we've got to compete. Canadians must learn that there is no free lunch."

As this is written there are still no estimates of the cost of the recent Gulf War to the Canadian taxpayer, but we know it will be large. Aside from the direct expenses of sending our own forces, we early on pledged $77 million to Turkey, Jordan and Egypt. Before the first missile was fired, the buildup had cost the U.S. government $30 billion, and $1 billion a day after the war began on January 16 is a low estimate. President George Bush, who had already put the American taxpayer on the hook for more than $500 billion for the savings and loan fiasco and for unknown amounts to bail out other banks caught up in Ronald Reagan's "voodoo economics," said, "Whatever the cost is we're going to have to pay it." For some things there appears to be plenty of money.

In Canada, then, the problem can be redefined as not the deficit or debt as such but an approach to the deficit in which it is expenditures that touch essential Canadian interests that must be scrapped rather than ones that are to the immediate advantage of the government's business clients. As has been amply demonstrated elsewhere (notably by Neil Brooks and Linda McQuaig), the government's handling of the tax system reflects similar thinking. If the federal government cannot and will not act to mitigate the effects of the business cycle, maintain key sectors of the economy, meet vital social needs or strengthen the tenuous links that make this one country, it is hardly surprising if many Canadians, in Quebec and elsewhere, begin to ask themselves whether we really need such a government. And so, as we try to develop more democratic procedures of government and a constitutional framework that more accurately corresponds to what Canada is, we also have to rethink the country's priorities for government spending and its forms of government intervention in the economy.

No one should underestimate the difficulty of actually implementing such a program. But working towards these goals is likely to be far more productive than simply perpetuating the paralysis that characterizes our politics today, especially at the federal level. Our present path is leading towards dissolution. We will have a democratic, binational Canada with a state structure capable of acting in the collective interests of its citizens, or we will in all probability have no Canada at all.

Sources

As noted in the preface, the information on which this book is based comes primarily from public sources. In this note on sources, we highlight some of the works that we found most useful in the preparation of each chapter. A fuller list of sources with complete bibliographical references follows.

Chapter 1: The Crisis of Canada's Existence

Jo Davis, ed., *Not a Sentimental Journey*, provides a lively pastiche of the controversy over the Via Rail cuts. The extensive and wideranging debate in English Canada on free trade is reflected in our previous book, *Selling Out*.

Chapter 2: The Natural Governing Party (1945-1957)

While the bulk of our sources are in perodical and newspaper files of the period, J.L Granatstein's books, *The Ottawa Men* and *Canada's War*, were particularly useful. J.L. Finlay and D.N. Sprague, *The Structure of Canadian History*, and Donald Creighton, *The Forked Road*, also provided valuable material on this period.

Many writers allege Liberal activity on behalf of the CCF in the 1942 York South byelection, suggesting that this was decisive in the Conservative defeat. However, the most decisive result of the defeat was the emergence of a new modern Conservative political agenda for the postwar period. This theme is developed in Timothy Colton's biography of Frederick Gardiner, *Big Daddy*.

The significance of the postwar Quebec-Ottawa struggle over income taxes is described in Paul-André Linteau et al., *Quebec Since 1930*.

Chapter 3: Three Faces of Nationalism (1957-1968)

Tom Kent's memoir, *A Public Purpose*, and Denis Smith's biography of Walter Gordon, *Gentle Patriot*, deal extensively with the fall and rise of the Liberal Party during this period, as does Walter Gordon's own *A Political Memoir*.

George Ball's predictions seem to have been borne out by time and events, and now two other American futurologists seem willing to put us out of our misery over the next decade by incorporating most of English Canada into the United States and leaving Quebec independent. See Marvin Cetron and Owen Davis, *The American Renaissance*.

While he buys into the absurd notion that although John Diefenbaker had been prime minister for three years before John F. Kennedy assumed office nobody in either the State Department or the American embassy in Ottawa knew how to pronounce Diefenbaker's name, Knowton Nash's *Kennedy and Diefenbaker* provides background to the feud between the two men.

Gad Horowitz, *Canadian Labour in Politics*, provides valuable insight into the forming of the NDP, as does David Lewis's memoir, *The Good Fight*.

André Laurendeau's *Journal* is a wise and perceptive observer's reflections on relations between French and English Canada at the time, and his observations apply to our own time as well.

The CBC's excellent documentary series *The Tenth Decade* gives a vivid sense of the Diefenbaker-Pearson era.

Chapter 4: Pierre Trudeau's Three-Quarter Turn (1968-1984)

Stephen Clarkson in his *Canada and the Reagan Challenge* provides the best and most complete overview of the complex economic relations with the United States during this whole period. Other prominent sources were Ron Graham's *One-Eyed Kings*, Richard Gwyn *The 49th Paradox* and Christina McCall-Newman *Grits*.

Clarkson and McCall's *Trudeau and Our Times*, vol. 1, provides a highly readable account of the constitutional struggle of 1980-82. Volume 2 of this work, expected in the fall of 1991, should round out these writers' picture of the Trudeau era.

Donald Brittain's classic film *The Champions* gives a particular flavour and immediacy of the conflict between Pierre Trudeau and René Lévesque on Quebec and Canada.

Chapter 5: The 1980s: The Corporate Decade

Apart from Richard J. Barnet and Ronald E. Müller's 1974 book *Global Reach*, it is only recently that substantial works on the global economy have begun to appear. The publications of Kenichi Ohmae and Robert Reich are among the most valuable.

In our previous books, notably *Winners, Losers* and *Brian Mulroney*, we have tried to describe the ongoing split in the Progressive Conservative Party. The latter book also discusses Mulroney's then very ambivalent position on policy issues within the party. Jeffrey Simpson's *Discipline of Power* is the most thorough examination of Joe Clark's brief time in power.

A full account of the historic attraction of the United States for Quebec is given in Robert Chodos and Eric Hamovitch, *Quebec and the American Dream*.

Chapter 6: In the Wake of the Free Trade Agreement

A particularly valuable source throughout, but especially in areas of multinational economic dealings, has been the work of David Crane, economics editor of the Toronto *Star*.

The most thorough dissection of the Meech Lake Accord is in Andrew Cohen, *A Deal Undone*.

Chapter 7: Beyond the Nation-State

Gerald Caplan, Michael Kirby and Hugh Segal's collaboration, *Election*, illustrates how the NDP was spooked by free trade, how the Liberals were spooked by John Turner, and how the 1988 election was torn out of the handlers' hands for a brief period. However the most valuable source on the election was produced by Allan Frizzell, Jon Pammett and Anthony Westell. Their *The Canadian General Election of 1988* gives a statistical overview of the election.

Chapter 8: Omens of a New Politics

Background to the current state of the NDP is provided in Gad Horowitz, *Canadian Labour in Politics*, Judy Steed, *Ed Broadbent*, and Hugh G. Thorburn, ed., *Party Politics in Canada*, 5th edition.

Chapter 9: The East Germany of North America?

In *Toward a Canada-Quebec Union*, Philip Resnick abandons the polemical tone of *Letters to a Québécois Friend* and gets back to what he does best, political analysis. Resnick comes to some of the same conclusions as the present writers, although by a somewhat different route.

Bibliography

Axworthy, Thomas S., and Trudeau, Pierre Elliott, eds. *Towards a Just Society: The Trudeau Years*. Toronto: Viking, 1990.

Ball, George. *The Discipline of Power*. Boston: Little, Brown, 1968.

Barnet, Richard J., and Müller, Ronald E. *Global Reach: The Power of the Multinational Corporations*. New York: Simon and Schuster, 1974.

Bissonnette, Lise. "Le disciple de Monnet: M. Bourassa n'évoque qu'un aspect de sa superstructure." Montreal *Le Devoir*, July 5, 1990.

Bothwell, Robert, and Kilbourn, William. *C.D. Howe: A Biography*. Toronto: McClelland and Stewart, 1979.

Bourassa, Robert. *Power from the North*. Toronto: Prentice-Hall, 1985.

Brooks, Neil, and McQuaig, Linda. "OK Michael Wilson, Here's the Alternative." *This Magazine*, December 1989, pp 15-20.

Brown, Patrick; Chodos, Robert; and Murphy, Rae. *Winners, Losers: The 1976 Tory Convention*. Toronto: Last Post/James Lorimer and Co., 1976.

Cameron, Duncan. "Crow Rates." *Canadian Forum*, September 1990, pp. 10-15.

Canada. Royal Commission on Bilingualism and Biculturalism. *Preliminary Report*. Ottawa: Queen's Printer, 1965.

--------. *Report*. Vol. 1. Ottawa: Queen's Printer, 1967.

Caplan, Gerald; Kirby, Michael; and Segal, Hugh. *Election: The Issues, the Strategies, the Aftermath*. Toronto: Prentice-Hall, 1989.

Cetron, Marvin, and Davis, Owen. *The American Renaissance*. New York: St. Martin's Press, 1989.

Chodos, Robert, and Hamovitch, Eric. *Quebec and the American Dream*. Toronto: Between the Lines, 1991.

Chodos, Robert; Murphy, Rae; and Hamovitch, Eric. *Selling Out: Four Years of the Mulroney Government.* Toronto: James Lorimer and Co., 1988.

Clarkson, Stephen. *Canada and the Reagan Challenge: Crisis and Adjustment 1981-85.* Toronto: James Lorimer and Co., 1985.

--------, and McCall, Christina. *Trudeau and Our Times.* Vol. 1: *The Magnificent Obsession.* Toronto: McClelland and Stewart, 1990.

Cohen, Andrew. *A Deal Undone: The Making and Breaking of the Meech Lake Accord.* Vancouver: Douglas and McIntyre, 1990.

Colton, Timothy. *Big Daddy: Frederick Gardiner.* Toronto: University of Toronto Press, 1980.

Creighton, Donald. *The Forked Road: Canada, 1939-1957.* Toronto: McClelland and Stewart, 1976.

Davis, Jo, ed. *Not a Sentimental Journey.* Goderich, Ont.: Gunbyfield Publishing, 1990.

Delacourt, Susan, and Fraser, Graham. "Marathon Talks Were All Part of Plan, PM Says." Toronto *Globe and Mail*, June 12, 1990.

Dufour, Christian. *A Canadian Challenge — Le défi québécois.* Translated by Heather Parker. Lantzville, B.C.: Oolichan Books/Halifax: Institute for Research on Public Policy, 1990.

--------. "A Problem That Rots the Entire Country." Toronto *Globe and Mail*, October 16, 1990.

Finlay, J.L., and Sprague, D.N. *The Structure of Canadian History.* Toronto: Prentice-Hall, 1979.

Fotheringham, Allan. "The Nearsighted Tory Incarnate." *Maclean's*, December 13, 1982.

Fraser, Graham. "Despite Polls, Tories Awed by Mulroney Morale Magic." Toronto *Globe and Mail*, April 14, 1990.

Frizzell, Allan; Pammett, Jon; and Westell, Anthony. *The Canadian General Election of 1988.* Ottawa: Carleton University Press, 1989.

Fullerton, Douglas. *Graham Towers and His Times.* Toronto: McClelland and Stewart, 1986.

"Goodbye to the Nation State?" *The Economist*, June 23, 1990, pp. 11-12.

Gordon, Walter. *A Political Memoir.* Toronto: McClelland and Stewart, 1977.

Graham, Ron. *One-Eyed Kings: Promise and Illusion in Canadian Politics.* Toronto: Collins, 1986.

Granatstein, J.L. *Canada's War: The Politics of the Mackenzie King Government, 1939-1945*. Toronto: Oxford University Press, 1975.

--------. *The Ottawa Men*. Toronto: Oxford University Press, 1982.

--------, and Bothwell, Robert. *Pirouette: Pierre Trudeau and Canadian Foreign Policy*. Toronto: University of Toronto Press, 1990.

Grant, George. *Lament for a Nation*. Toronto: McClelland and Stewart, 1965.

Gregg, Allan, and Posner, Michael. *The Big Picture: What Canadians Think about Almost Everything*. Toronto: Macfarlane Walter and Ross, 1990.

Gwyn, Richard. "Conservative Me-Tooism." Ottawa *Citizen*, January 12, 1984.

--------. *The 49th Paradox: Canada in North America* Toronto: McClelland and Stewart, 1985.

Hersh, Seymour. *The Price of Power*. New York: Summit Press, 1983.

Horowitz, Gad. *Canadian Labour in Politics*. Toronto: University of Toronto Press, 1968.

Hutchison, Bruce. *The Far Side of the Street*. Toronto: Macmillan, 1976.

Kennedy, Paul. *The Rise and Fall of the Great Powers*. New York: Random House, 1987.

Kent, Tom. *A Public Purpose*. Montreal: McGill-Queen's University Press, 1988.

Kierans, Eric, and Stewart, Walter. *Wrong End of the Rainbow: The Collapse of Free Enterprise in Canada*. Toronto: Collins, 1988.

King, William Lyon Mackenzie. *Industry and Humanity*. Reprint ed. Toronto: University of Toronto Press, 1973.

Latouche, Daniel. *Canada and Quebec, Past and Future: An Essay*. Toronto: University of Toronto Press, 1986.

--------. "May 20, 1980: Referendum." *Compass*, July 1990, pp. 14-17.

Laurendeau, André. *Journal tenu pendant la Commission royale d'enquête sur le bilinguisme et le biculturalisme*. Montreal: VLB Éditeur/Le Septentrion, 1990.

Lee, Robert Mason. *One Hundred Monkeys: The Triumph of Popular Wisdom in Canadian Politics*. Toronto: Macfarlane Walter and Ross, 1989.

Lewis, David. *The Good Fight*. Toronto: McClelland and Stewart, 1981.

Linteau, Paul-André; Durocher, René; Robert, Jean-Claude; and Ricard, François. *Quebec Since 1930.* Translated by Robert Chodos and Ellen Garmaise. Toronto: James Lorimer and Co., 1991.

Lipset, Seymour Martin. *Continental Divide: The Values and Institutions of the United States and Canada.* New York: Routledge, 1990.

Lisée, Jean-François. *In the Eye of the Eagle.* Translated by Arthur Holden, Kathe Rothe, and Claire Rothman. Toronto: Harper-Collins, 1990.

"Looking around for Ideas." Interview with Robert Bourassa. *Time,* Canadian edition, July 9, 1990, pp. 12-13.

McCall-Newman, Christina. *Grits: An Intimate Potrait of the Liberal Party.* Toronto: Macmillan, 1982.

McDonald, Lynn. *The Party That Changed Canada: The New Democratic Party Then and Now.* Toronto: Macmillan, 1987.

Mackie, G.R. "Future Transportation." Letters to the Editor, Toronto *Globe and Mail,* August 28, 1989.

Magocsi, Paul. "The Era of the Nation-State Is Over." *Compass,* March-April 1991, pp. 13-15.

Marsh, Leonard. *Report on Social Security for Canada.* Reprint ed. Toronto: University of Toronto Press, 1975.

Mathews, Georges. *Quiet Resolution: Quebec's Challenge to Canada.* Translated by Dominique Clift. Toronto: Summerhill Press, 1990.

Melnyk, George. "From CCF to NDP to...." *Compass,* November 1989, pp. 40-43.

Mossber, Walter S. "New 'One-Worlders' Are Conservatives." *Wall Street Journal,* April 3, 1989.

Murphy, Rae; Chodos, Robert; and Auf der Maur, Nick. *Brian Mulroney: The Boy from Baie-Comeau.* Toronto: James Lorimer and Co., 1984.

Murphy, Rae, and Sinclair, Scott. "Mission to Mexico." *This Magazine,* June 1990, pp. 10-13.

Nash, Knowlton. *Kennedy and Diefenbaker: Fear and Loathing across the Undefended Border.* Toronto: McClelland and Stewart, 1990.

Newman, Peter C. *The Distemper of Our Times.* Toronto: McClelland and Stewart, 1968.

Nolan, Brian. *King's War: Mackenzie King and the Politics of War, 1939-1945.* Toronto: Random House, 1988.

Ohmae, Kenichi. *The Borderless World.* Toronto: Harper-Collins, 1990.

Oliver, Michael. "The Quebec Challenge." *Canadian Forum*, March 1990, pp. 27-28.

Pickersgill, J.W. *My Years with Louis St. Laurent*. Toronto: University of Toronto Press, 1975.

Progressive Conservative Party of Canada. "The Last Straw: Report of the Task Force on Rail Passenger Service." Ottawa, 1981. Mimeo.

"Quebec 1990: What Now?" A symposium. *Compass*, July 1990, pp. 18-34.

The Quebec Referendum: What Happened and What Next? A Dialogue the Day after with Claude Forget and Daniel Latouche, May 21, 1980. Cambridge, Mass.: University Consortium for Research on North America, 1980.

Picard, André. "Quebec Mohawks to Be 'Nation within a State.'" Toronto *Globe and Mail*, January 6, 1990.

Reich, Robert B. *The Work of Nations: Preparing Ourselves for 21st-Century Capitalism*. New York: Alfred A. Knopf, 1991.

Rémillard, Gil. "Notes pour l'allocution du ministre de la justice et ministre des affaires intergouvernementales canadiennes du Québec, Gil Rémillard, à l'occasion de son acceptation d'un doctorat 'honoris causa' à l'Université d'Aix-Marseille III, le 14 mai 1990." Mimeo.

Resnick, Philip. *Letters to a Québécois Friend*. With a reply by Daniel Latouche. Montreal: McGill-Queen's University Press, 1990.

--------. *Toward a Canada-Quebec Union*. Montreal: McGill-Queen's University Press, 1991.

Scott, F.R. "W.L.M.K." In *The Collected Poems of F.R. Scott*, pp. 78-79. Toronto: McClelland and Stewart, 1981.

Simpson, Jeffrey. *Discipline of Power*. Toronto: Personal Library, 1980.

--------. *Spoils of Power: The Politics of Patronage*. Toronto: Collins, 1988.

Smith, Denis. *Gentle Patriot: A Political Biography of Walter Gordon*. Edmonton: Hurtig Publishers, 1973.

Sprague, D.N. *Post-Confederation Canada: The Structure of Canadian History since 1867*. Toronto: Prentice-Hall, 1990.

Steed, Judy. *Ed Broadbent: The Pursuit of Power*. Toronto: Viking, 1988.

Swift, Jamie. *Odd Man Out: The Life and Times of Eric Kierans*. Vancouver: Douglas and McIntyre, 1988.

Taylor, Charles. "A Free, Independent Quebec in a Strong, United Canada." *Compass*, May 1990, pp. 46-48.

52/

Thorburn, Hugh G., ed. *Party Politics in Canada*. 5th edition. Toronto: Prentice-Hall, 1985.

Vastel, Michel. "Bleu, rouge...ou vert?" *L'Actualité*, May 15, 1990, pp. 32-40.

--------. *The Outsider: The Life of Pierre Elliott Trudeau*. Translated by Hubert Bauch. Toronto: Macmillan, 1990.

Watkins, Mel. "Once More unto the Meech: A Final Assault on the Accord." *This Magazine*, April-May 1990, pp. 14-16.

Westell, Anthony. "Trudeau's Grand Design: More Chaos than Conspiracy." Toronto *Star*, January 2, 1976.

White, Randall. *Fur Trade to Free Trade: Putting the Canada-U.S. Trade Agreement in Historical Perspective*. Toronto: Dundern, 1988.

Wilson, H.T. *Retreat from Governance: Canada and the Continental-International Challenge*. Hull: Voyageur, 1989.

Woodcock, George. "Five-Year Fascism." *Canadian Forum*, December 1990, pp. 16-18.

--------. "Why Can't We Throw the Rascals Out?" Toronto *Globe and Mail*, October 3, 1990.

York, Geoffrey. "Old Ways Guide Native Leaders." Toronto *Globe and Mail*, June 21, 1990.

Zachary, Adam. "Ottawa Goes One for Two." *This Magazine*, July 1987, pp. 4-5.

--------. "Natives Say 'We Killed Meech Lake.'" *This Magazine*, September 1990, pp. 4-5.